FACTUAL PERSUASION

CHANGING THE MINDS OF ISLAM'S SUPPORTERS

BILL WARNER

CENTER FOR THE STUDY OF
POLITICAL ISLAM

FACTUAL PERSUASION

CHANGING THE MINDS OF ISLAM'S SUPPORTERS

BILL WARNER

CENTER FOR THE STUDY OF
POLITICAL ISLAM

COPYRIGHT © 2011 CSPI, LLC

ISBN13   978-1-936659-14-2

PUBLISHED BY CSPI, LLC
WWW.CSPIPUBLISHING.COM

PRINTED IN THE USA

TABLE OF CONTENTS

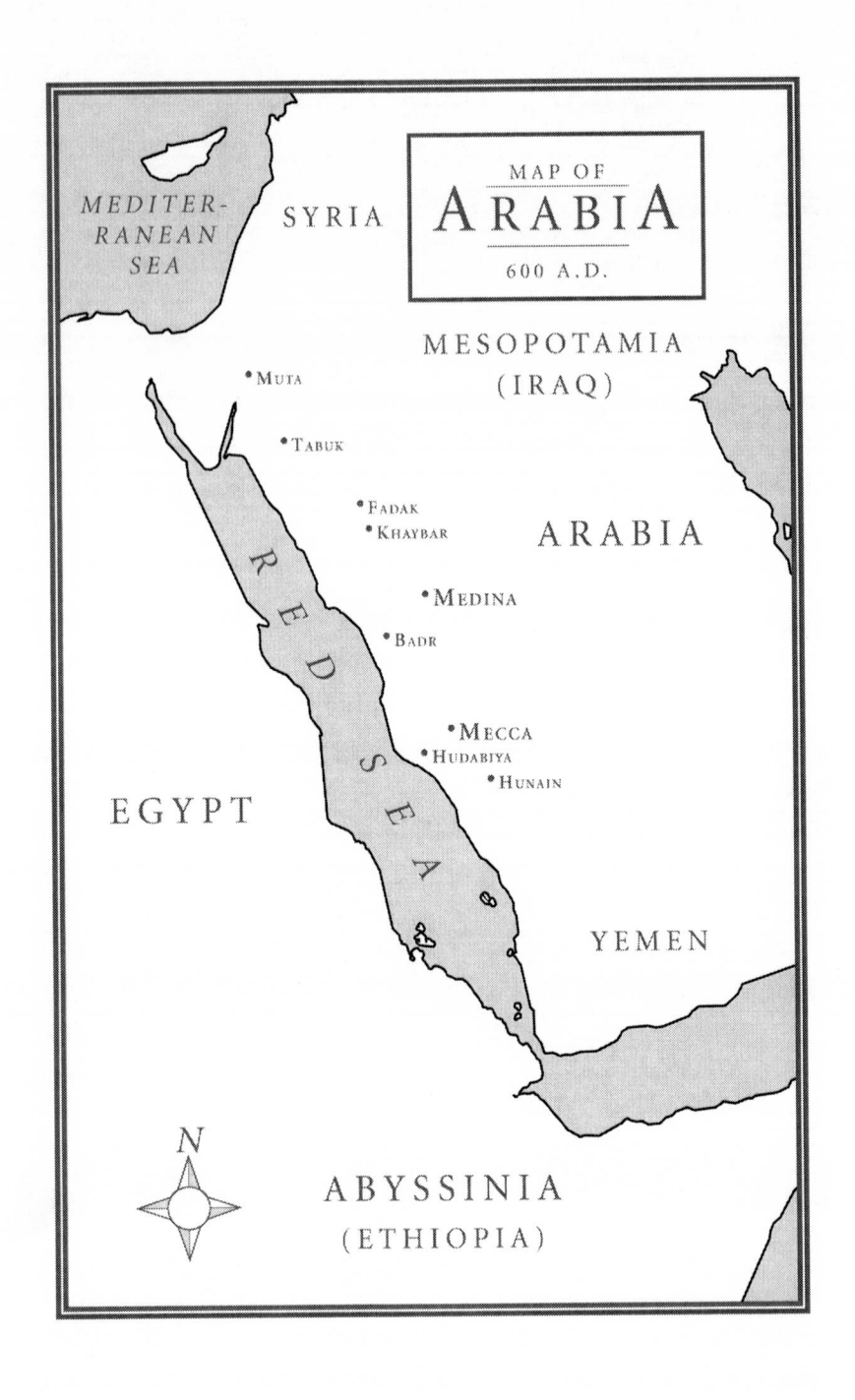

THE CONFUSION OF ISLAM

Chapter 1

FOREWORD

This is a how-to book about persuading people about the true nature of Islam. The method that is taught here is based upon understanding Islam's doctrine as found in three texts, the Trilogy: Koran, Sira (the biography of Mohammed) and Hadith (his traditions). The Trilogy contains the complete foundation of Islamic doctrine.

This book is intended for those whose have read the Trilogy. What you have learned from reading the Trilogy can be the most effective tool of persuasion you can have, but you need to see how the tool is actually applied and used.

Since you might have this book and never have read the Trilogy, here are a few short definitions of terms and concepts that you must know to follow the reasoning.

Kafir—a Kafir is a non-Muslim.

Sunna—Mohammed is the perfect Muslim. His practice (works and words, Sunna) are the perfect pattern of the sacred life.

Sharia—Sharia is Islamic law based on the Koran and the Sunna of Mohammed.

Dhimmi—dhimmi is used in two senses. The original dhimmis were defeated Jews who could worship, but had to live under Sharia law and pay high taxes. The second sense of the term is an apologist for Islam.

Dualism—Islam frequently has two contradicting manifestations. For instance, Islam is the religion of peace, but Islam is also the doctrine of jihad murder. Islam is both religiously tolerant and has a death sentence for leaving Islam. Under dualism both sides of the contradiction are equally true. Real Islam is both.

INTRODUCTION

Little of the talk in the media, religious circles and politics has anything to do with Islam and very much to do with political correctness, multiculturalism, and propaganda. Once you know the doctrine of Political Islam, you will see that the experts are long on opinion and short on actual facts. Articles and TV programs presented in the media give only a glancing look at the actual Islamic doctrine.

This book presents an fact-based approach to Islam that uses critical thought in order that you can reason and persuade others.

On September 11, 2001 it was not only the military and police who did not know what Islam was going to do. We found that our cultural institutions, which should have been able to explain why the attack happened, were also clueless. The attack on the World Trade Center caught everybody off guard.

The first words out of leadership's mouths declared that Islam was not to blame. No, Islam was the peaceful religion. Soon more apologies came from the media, politicians, professors, religious leaders and the pundits. These apologies were based on current social theory of political correctness and multiculturalism. However, in the background there was a muttering that Islam was the cause, not the victim. But anyone who would suggest any bad news about Islam had little support from the "authorities".

There have been many books written by those who try to bring the truth of Islam to the public's attention. All of them fall into the category of understanding Islam, knowing what Islam is and what it has done in the past and is doing today.

This book is about knowing and doing. You will know more and be able to argue, reason and debate about Political Islam. You can persuade in a calm assured manner. And you can do so up against the media expert, the college professor, the Muslim at work or your own religious leader. The reason you can always persuade is not due to some cleverness or deceit or intimidation. You can win because you have a secret weapon—knowledge. If you know the most about a subject, then you can always bring more pressure to bear in any discussion.

The first step in being able to persuade someone is to have a solid foundation about Islamic doctrine. The biggest "fog of war" in dealing with Islam is the confusion about what it is. Try asking someone: "What is Islam?" and you will get a myriad of answers. But, there is an exact, fact-based answer to the question.

Once you scientifically define Islam, its political nature can be recognized and separated. It is the political purpose of Islam to annihilate all other civilizations. Those who should guard us from destruction are not understanding this threat of annihilation, so we as individuals must do the job.

HOW NOT TO STUDY ISLAM

The media has developed a unique form of writing. Page after page is filled with words, but what is the basis for these statements? The answer is that they are opinions, personal opinions. The media's comments on Islam are based on hearsay with little or no factual data.

Possibly the worst source about Islam comes from famous people. They spout some personal opinion like "I know a Muslim. He is a nice person. Islam is peaceful." Presidents, bishops, senators, governors, generals and that eternal source of true knowledge—a star from Hollywood or a rock band—all hand out the same ignorant arguments. Here is an example by the Dalai Lama:

> "Nowadays to some people the Muslim tradition appears more militant," the 70-year-old exiled monk said at a weekend conference, which aimed to bring Muslims and Buddhists together.
> "I feel that's totally wrong. Muslims, like any other traditions—same message, same practice. That is a practice of compassion," he said.[1]

His comments are pure opinion and he does not offer any factual basis for his words. He asks us to believe him because he is the Dalai Lama.

There is a special category of comments called "not the real Islam". Whenever an aspect of Islam is unpleasant, the immediate apologist comment is: "that is not the real Islam." But the more common treatment of any unpleasant event is to simply ignore it. At the time of this writing, there have been hundreds of attacks by jihadists around the world, but only a very few are reported, and there is there any connecting of the dots or finding a pattern of behavior. So here we have another characteristic of reporting on Islam—it is never systematic.

The great bulk of the media and Muslims mouthed a few platitudes: Islam is a religion based upon the Koran; a few "extremist Muslims" have hijacked the religion; "moderate Muslims" will solve the problems of Islam; Islam just needs to be reformed, the "bad stuff" is only a matter of interpretation. But notice something about these apologies: there are no

---

1.http://www.cbsnews.com/stories/2006/04/16/national/main1501186.
shtml?source=RSS&attr=U.S._1501186, San Francisco, April 16, 2006, William Vitka

facts to support the assertions. (Quoting a Koran verse is the very weakest form of presenting facts. We will see later why dualism makes this almost meaningless.) Pseudo-facts that quote the opinion of some scholar with an Arabic name serve as the basis of most articles.

Then there are the articles by Muslim scholars who praise Islam as the only driving force in the world. Indeed, they never reveal the slightest doubt about the doctrine of Islam as an absolute truth. Inside of Islam, there is so little critical thinking that it is a good approximation to say that critical thought does not exist. Self-doubt does not exist among Muslim thinkers either. This turns out to be a clue as to the true nature of Islamic doctrine.

Islam's public image is "Islam is the religion of peace." There are two things wrong with that statement. The worst error in thinking about Islam is that it is a religion. As you will see later, religion is the smallest part of Islam. Islam as a religion is of no consequence to anyone except a Muslim. Islam is an entirely separate civilization. The most important part of Islamic doctrine turns out to be political. Mohammed had no success with Islam until he made it a political system.

Knowledge knows what is, but wisdom can see what is not. There is an enormous gap in our knowledge about Islam. Look at these simple facts. North Africa and Egypt used to be Christian. North Africa was European. Syria, Lebanon, Iraq, and the rest of the Middle East were Christian. Turkey used to be Greek Anatolia. Afghanistan and all of the rest of the Silk Route countries were Buddhist. Pakistan and Bangladesh used to be Buddhist and Hindu. Today all of those nations are Islamic. Did Islam "just happen" or was there a process that took centuries? How did Greek Christian Anatolia become Islamic Turkey? The history of Islamification is a non-history. It does not exist according to our "experts".

Why are all of the Muslim thinkers so sure about Islam while non-Muslims are so confused? Why does it seem so simple to them and so muddled to us? Why is it that an illiterate Egyptian peasant can understand Islam, but the Western university professor cannot?

A FOUNDATIONAL APPROACH

We need a fact-based approach to Islam, not opinions. We need a rational method that gives the same results, no matter who uses it. Notice that the opinion-based method gives different answers depending upon who is asking the questions.

We need a method that does not depend upon censorship. The cultural/political climate of today does not allow arguments or debate. Any views that differ from the multicultural "we are all one big happy family where everyone is the same as everybody else and all cultures are equally valid" are called bigoted, racist and hateful.

We need a method of study that encourages argument. That means that we need critical thinking. Today critical thinking is condemned since it involves looking at all sides of a question. Currently, in our culture, any position that violates the multicultural model is declared evil. Instead we are supposed to view the government/university/media position as the Truth-From-Above.

Islam is based on Allah and the Sunna of Mohammed. Allah is found in the Koran. The Sunna is the perfect example of Mohammed's every word and deed. The Sunna is is found in the Sira (his biography) and the Hadith (his traditions). The Koran, Sira and Hadith are called the Trilogy and contain the entire religious and political doctrine of Islam. The Trilogy is published by CSPI and it is assumed that you have read these books, since all the arguments presented here are based on the doctrine found in the Trilogy.

OFFICIAL ISLAM

Chapter 2

INTRODUCTION

This book is devoted to exploring the true nature of Islam as revealed in its sacred texts and its history. There is another Islam that was given voice by George Bush, Obama and the media. Bush laid down a basic version of Official Islam in the National Cathedral soon after 9/11. Obama added many details in his Cairo speech, June 4, 2009.

But Official Islam was not invented by the media, Bush or Obama, but by the Muslim Brotherhood[1]. This doctrine became the standard in all of the universities when the Brotherhood, powered by Saudi money, invaded and took over the Middle East departments. That is the reason that the media went along with the official version. This is what they were all taught. The preachers, rabbis and all the politicians believe in this Official Islam, at least in public.

OFFICIAL ISLAM

Here are the major points of Official Islam:

- Islam is a religion similar to Christianity and Judaism. They all worship the same god and are of the Abrahamic faith.
- Good Muslims prove that Islam is good
- There are no jihadists, just extremists fueled by poverty
- "Extremists" cause the violence
- The "bad stuff" in the Koran is due to how it is interpreted
- Islam must be accommodated in as many ways as possible
- One of the proofs of Islam's greatness is the Islamic Golden Age, thought by some to be humanity's best days
- Violence is perpetrated by Muslims because they are poor and abused

---

1   The Muslim Brotherhood is a underground organization devoted to the rule of Sharia over the world. They have been active in the US since 1960.

- The West received the foundation of its intellectual world from Islam
- The Crusades were a great evil committed by Christians
- There are mostly moderate Muslims and only a few extremist Muslims
- Islam is only found in the Koran
- Good Muslims will reform the "extremists"
- Islam is the religion of tolerance
- Islam has a Golden Rule
- Islam is a wonderful part of American culture
- Islam is the religion of freedom and justice

But the official version of Islam is a Big Lie[2]. The fact that the Official Islam does not agree with the Koran, Sira and Hadith is of no importance, since it is not based upon them. Official Islam is based upon the propaganda of our establishment media, government and schools. Not one line of the Official Islam is totally true and many of the points are complete fabrications.

At best, some assertions are partially true. A half-truth is a lie. When you testify in our courts you have to swear an oath:

"I swear to tell the whole truth and nothing but the truth."

Official Islam is not provable and is delivered by "authorities". This book is based upon critical/scientific thought. The Official Islam is based upon authoritarian thought—that is, you must believe it because those who have more power than you have say that it is true. Official Islam is a mind-set of denial and delusion and is the intellectual basis of the destruction of our civilization.

Official Islam is refuted in Chapter 6.

---

2   Adolf Hitler, *Mein Kampf,* Houghton Mifflin Co., Boston, MA, 1971, pgs. 231, 232.

CAN'T WE ALL JUST GET ALONG?

Chapter 4

INTRODUCTION

Kafirs have a basic instinct when faced with Islam—let's make some compromises. We will do things your way, Islam can reform and life will be good. This will not work and has never worked, but Kafirs refuse to be logical and study Islam to see why compromise won't work.

We must go through all of the steps of compromise to see why they will fail. In particular, we must see why reform is a logical impossibility. And last, but not least, we must see why the "good" Muslim cannot and will not help to achieve a solution.

The elites tell us that Islam has always been part of one big happy human family. Islam is here and it is a wonderful thing. Islam is a foundational part of our civilization. Muslims make wonderful neighbors.

The elites tell us that if we don't get along with Political Islam, if we find a problem, then the problem is with us. The fact of the matter is that Mohammed attacked every single neighbor he had. His only success came through violence. His dying words were to hurt Jews, Christians and all Kafirs. Mohammed was Islam and he was never compatible with any Kafir. The Big Lie is just that. There is no way to live with Islam. Life with Islam is a succession of demands. Mohammed never stopped until 100% of his demands were met. That was life with Mohammed—the Sunna.

Islam is a civilization that is designed to extinguish all Kafir civilizations down to their last cultural vestige. Annihilation is Sunna. Mohammed did not stop until the Kafirs surrendered to his demands to change the smallest details of their lives into his way of doing. The last 1400 years of history is proof of the brutal efficiency of Islamic politics. There has never been a culture where Islam and Kafirs existed in long-term peace. After a long enough time period, Islam takes over the civilization. This is the goal of Islam.

But since Kafirs don't know anything about the history of Islam, they think that we will work this out like we always have. We will find a compromise. After all, in Kafir civilization, progress is made through teamwork and compromise. The first and crucial error is thinking that Islam is analogous to our civilization and that our rules apply to it. Let's compare Islam with our civilization's ideals.

Freedom Of Expression

First, the ideal citizen of Islam has no freedom, but is a slave of Allah and the Sunna. Freedom of expression means you can disagree with Islam.

Mohammed laid the perfect example of freedom of expression when he finally gained power in Mecca. In the beginning when he had no power in Mecca, he allowed argument about his doctrine. After he was driven out of Mecca and later returned as its conqueror, he issued death warrants against all of those who had disagreed with him. When Mohammed died, there was not a single person left in Arabia who disagreed with him. Intellectual subservience to Mohammed/Islam was total. The Sharia denies freedom of expression. Islam tolerates discussion of Islam only when it is getting started and is politically weak.

Freedom Of Religion

If you are a Muslim and want to leave Islam, you become an apostate. An Islamic apostate can be killed. An apostate is even a worse creature than a Kafir. The Koran says that apostasy is a crime worse than mass murder.

But doesn't Islam preach that Christians, Jews and Muslims are all members of the Abrahamic faith? Is that not freedom of religion? In Islam the only real Christians and Jews are dhimmis since they must declare their own scriptures to be corrupt and that Mohammed is the last prophet of both Jews and Christians. Those who don't are not true Christians and Jews, but Kafirs.

And what about the atheists, Buddhists, Hindus, Jains, and on and on? They are all hated Kafirs just like Christians and Jews.

If there is freedom of religion, explain how every Muslim country becomes 100% Islamic eventually? Explain this in terms of freedom or tolerance.

Slavery

The Koran sanctions and encourages slavery. Mohammed was the perfect slave owner, slave wholesaler, slave retailer, slave torturer and sex slave user. Even though Islam sold Americans every slave, Islam has never acknowledged this fact nor apologized.

Criticism

In our culture, we have the ability to criticize our own actions and the actions of our political and religious leaders and correct mistakes. Criticism of Islamic religion or politics by Muslims is rare and can be life-threatening.

Freedom of the Press

Due to the publication of the Danish Mohammed cartoons, buildings were burned, people were killed, and almost no newspaper would reprint these political cartoons. You can say anything you want about Islam as long as Islam is not offended. Freedom of the press is forbidden in Sharia law. Sharia blasphemy laws prohibit criticism, or even asking questions, about Islamic doctrine.

Diversity

Islam is the supreme mono-culture, dedicated to abolishing all other cultures. There is no multiculturalism in Islam. After Islam takes over the host culture devolves into some form of Islam. Where is the Buddhist culture of Afghanistan? the Coptic culture of Egypt? the Berber culture of North Africa? the Christian culture of Iraq? the Zoroastrian culture of Iran? They have all been annihilated.

Equal Justice Under the Law

The Koran specifically says that justice is served with different penalties for Muslims and Kafirs. A Muslim is not to be killed in retaliation for killing a Kafir. A Kafir may not testify against a Muslim in Islamic law. The entire Sharia law is based upon one set of laws for Muslims and another set of laws for Kafirs.

Ethics

Our ethics are based upon the Golden Rule, with all peoples considered as equal "others". Islam is based upon dualistic ethics, with one set of rules for Muslims and another set of rules for Kafirs. Kafirs are hated by Allah and are targeted for annihilation by Mohammed. Kafirs must be subjugated. Islamic ethics are dualistic—Muslims are treated well and Kafirs are treated as second-class citizens or worse, if it is deemed necessary to Islam.

Women

In Islam, women are subjugated to the males. In court they are treated as half of a man and they are equal only on Judgment Day. Both the Sunna and the Koran say that wives can be and should be beaten. The Sharia even lays out the precise procedure for wife-beating.

Torture

Torture is allowed in the Sunna and the Koran recommends cutting off of hands and feet and crucifying Kafirs. Mohammed repeatedly tortured Kafirs, even to death. Torture of Kafirs is Sunna.

Separation of Church and State

Our Constitution separates the church and state, but Islam demands that religion and state be combined as one unit. Sharia law includes both religious law and secular without distinction. Islam is a theocracy.

Friendship

Surely friendship is one of the most basic aspects of being human. But Mohammed was never the friend of a Kafir. His uncle, Abu Talib, adopted him, raised him, taught his business trade and protected him from harm by the Meccans. When he died a Kafir, Mohammed's first words were to condemn him to Hell. There are 12 verses in the Koran that say that a Muslim is not the friend of a Kafir.

Human Rights

There are no human rights in Islam, because there is no humanity in the Koran, just believers and Kafirs. Kafirs have no rights. Kafirs are hated by Allah and are lower than animals.

Since Islam does not have a point of agreement with our civilization, there is no way to find any compromise. Islam is not part of our civilization and does not play by our rules. When we try to use our rules, we always lose. How do you compromise with a civilization based on the principles of submission and duality?

REFORM?

The magical thinking of many intellectuals is that Islam can be reformed, like Christianity and Judaism experienced. This sounds great. Islam changes its ways and settles down to live among fellow humans.

Only this will not work. It is impossible to reform Islam, because it was designed so it could not be reformed or changed.

Why do we want to reform Islam? Do we care if Muslims pray three times a day, instead of five times? No. The only reason we want reform is because of the violence against us. We do not want to reform the religion of Islam; we want to reform Political Islam.

THE PROBLEMS OF REFORM

The Koran is perfect, complete and universal. The Koran says that Mohammed is the perfect model of a Muslim. The first problem is the perfection of the Trilogy—a perfect Koran and a perfect Sunna. How do you reform perfection? Why would Muslims want to improve perfection? If you take something out of the Koran, was the item you removed imperfect? If so, then the Koran was not perfect. Do you see the problem with reforming perfection?

The other problem with reformation is the amount of detail in the Sunna. The Sira is 800 pages long and Mohammed is on every page. Then there are the 6800 hadiths in Bukhari. The amount of Sunna is vast and covers the smallest detail, down to how many times to breathe when you drink a glass of water.

There is too much material for the doctrine to be reformed. For instance, 67% of Mohammed's prophetic career is about jihad[1]; it is not as if you can turn a blind eye to a few items and achieve reformation. Cutting out 67% of the Sira does not reform it, but creates an entire new text.

And Islam will never eliminate the one concept that has brought it success, jihad. All of Islam's success has been based upon political submission, dualism and violence. What the Kafirs want changed is the violence, pressure, arguing and politics. Demanding the Kafirs' submission and using violence works for Islam. The violence, pressure, arguments and demands are not going to stop because they have worked for 1400 years and are working better today than any time in the past.

---

1   http://cspipublishing.com/statistical/TrilogyStats/Percentage_of_Trilogy_Text_Devoted_to_Jihad.html

THE GOOD MUSLIM

There is an attempt to make the problem of Islam go away. It is the "good Muslim" who will save the day. Everybody seems to know a "good Muslim" who is a friend at work.

What is a good Muslim? A good Muslim is one who seems non-violent. But that point of view is not Islamic. Islam is the one and only basis of determining what a good Muslim is. An apologist's opinion of "good" is not relevant to anyone, except to the apologist and his friends. Islam says that a good Muslim is one who follows the Koran and the Sunna. That is the one and only criteria of being a good Muslim.

Apologists think that good Muslims are a proof of a "good" Islam and that the doctrine makes no difference. Oddly enough, Muslims do not agree with this. Muslims have one and only one definition of what a "good Muslim" is, one who has submitted to Islam and follows the Sunna. The cause is Islam; the effect is Muslim. Apologists think that Islam submits to Muslims, but apologists are ignorant, so they are free of facts, and in the soil of ignorance, any fantastic flower grows.

The problem in talking about Muslims as a group of people is that there are three kinds of Muslim. The first kind is the Meccan Muslim. A Meccan Muslim is primarily a religious person without the jihadic politics. A Medinan Muslim is a political Muslim. Then there is the Muslim who follows the Golden Rule, instead of Islamic ethics.

At this point a voice can be heard: "I know this Muslim and he is a good person. There are good Muslims." Notice the shift from Islam to a person. Yes, he may be a good person, but that is different from being a good Muslim. His goodness is due to his following the Golden Rule and treating a Kafir as a human being.

A Golden Rule Muslim is one who is an apostate to some degree. Maybe the Golden Rule Muslim drinks beer or doesn't go to the mosque. All Muslims have some Kafir in them. The Kafir civilization has much to offer: freedom, wealth, friendship, women who do not wear a bag for a garment and great entertainment. Some Muslims prefer Kafir civilization to Islamic civilization in many ways.

Since every Muslim can have three parts, it is hard to nail him down. There is a shifty quality that goes with the territory. Which center of gravity is he coming from? Is he religious, political, or friend? If religious or political, then he is not your friend, but a deceiver. But if he is your friend, then he is following the Golden Rule and is a Kafir. But how do you ever trust him? When is he Kafir? When is he Muslim?

COMPROMISE

Tolerance always seeks some form of negotiated compromise. Both sides give a little and come up with a solution that both can live with. It tacitly assumes honest discussions and fairness. Tolerance also assumes equality between the persons, parties or groups. None of these criteria are met with any negotiations between Muslims and Kafirs. Islam has no compromises to make. Islam is perfect and has nothing to learn or adopt from Kafir civilization. The Islamic positions are perfect because they are based upon the Sunna of Mohammed. A compromise with Kafirs is a compromise with evil and ignorance.

Mohammed always pressed his neighbors for more and more accommodations, and in the end, he always got what he wanted. In the end, Mohammed achieved 100% of all of his demands. There was only one time he compromised. At a certain point in his career, Mohammed compromised with the polytheists and agreed that their gods had some power to guide. Then the Koran spoke against this idea and said that Satan had planted this idea (the Satanic verses). [This event was the basis of Salman Rusdie's novel, *The Satanic Verses*. That novel won his a death fatwah.] It was the only error Mohammed ever made during his rise to complete power. He never compromised again.

Accommodation and submission has never worked with Islam—never. But that is the only solution we try and as a result, each day Kafirs become less free.

WHY WE LOSE

Islam has expanded since its first inception. We have decided to not oppose its growth, since that would be bigoted. In our present mind-set, there is nothing to stop Islam from prevailing. Europe is rapidly being overtaken by Muslim immigration and high birth rates. The problem is that Europe's elites and governments are fully accommodated to the end of European civilization and the beginning of Eurabia. European media, intellectuals and government officials only want to help the process of the death of Europe by assisting Islam and yielding to all of Political Islam's demands, including ever more welfare and immigration.

We agree to suspend the use of critical thinking and not study or critique Islam's political doctrine. All of the thinking is done for us. Are you afraid of Islam? Accept the Official Islam of the apologists and you will feel better. We may have to make some accommodations for things like Sharia law, but we have a happy surrender.

Ignorance is the official political point-of-view. No one who actually knows anything about the doctrine or history of Political Islam is ever given a place at forums or discussions. Knowing the truth disqualifies you from commenting.

Ignorance means that in all of our dealings with Political Islam, we will always make a decision based upon our ethics and our world-view, so we will always make the wrong decision. A classic example was America's "War on Terror". We decided to mount a military campaign against an enemy we named as terrorists. We declared that Muslims were just like us and that we would accommodate all of their demands while we battled terrorists.

Knowledge about Islam would have meant that our first question would have been: who is the enemy? Since the enemy is Political Islam, it means that we should have fought an ideological war, not a military war.

An ideological war would have meant that eight years after 9/11, every American Kafir would have been taught who Mohammed was, about the message of the Koran and the fact that we were all Kafirs. We would know how Sharia law contradicts every principle of our government. In short, by now we would know our enemy and what its nature is.

Instead, we find ways to blame ourselves for the problem of Political Islam. There are those mischievous jihadists, but they are not "real" Muslims. This form of self-loathing is supported by our ignorance in the realm of education. An audit of university curriculums shows that the following are not taught at any known public American university:

- The Tears of Jihad—the deaths of 270 million Kafirs over 1400 years
- The history of the dhimmi and dhimmitude
- The conquest of Christian/Hindu/Buddhist territory—Afghanistan, Pakistan, all the Silk Route countries, Turkey, Middle East, Egypt, North Africa and the rest of Africa
- How Sharia law impacts the lives of women
- The concept of the Kafir
- The Koran (in its entirety)
- The Sira (in its entirety)
- The Hadith (in its entirety)
- Islam's dualistic ethics and logic are not examined in philosophy
- Islamic slavery

What is taught about Islam is that it is one of the great world religions and that the high point of human civilization was the Islamic Golden Age in Baghdad and in Moorish Spain. Islamic poetry, architecture, and the Arabic language are studied, as well as modern Arabic history are viewed through a lens of political science and as a reaction to Western colonialism. Islam is not taught as an empire of conquest. The spread of Islam is taught as a wonderful benefit for the conquered Kafirs. The university courses never teach about any suffering at the hands of Islam.

You can get a degree in Middle East studies, become a diplomat in the Middle East and never read the Koran, Sira or Hadith. You will read some selections from this Trilogy, but there will be no systemic study of it. If you edit out the Jew-hatred from Hitler's *Mein Kampf*, then there is nothing offensive about it. In the same way, selective readings from the Koran, the Sira and Hadith can be very benign.

Since all of our responses are based upon official ignorance, our decisions are not based on reality and our plans fail. We lose to Islam once more.

SHAPING

Chapter 5

INTRODUCTION

Islam is such a foreign topic to most people that your first step should be to prepare the basis of the discussion. Most people have never heard much about Islam that makes sense. Look at the Koran. Who understands it? Most people figure that there is no rational basis for talking about Islam. Preparing a rational foundation gives you the advantage.

The most important aspect of persuading is teaching and explaining about Islamic doctrine. This means educating the other person as a student. However, presenting the facts is not enough. Political Islam is so far removed from Kafir civilization that it is strange. There is a tendency to deny the facts. The inner voice says, "That cannot be Islam. It cannot be that cruel. Muslims don't really believe that."

You are planting seeds and the ground must be prepared, exactly like a garden. The student's mind is filled with the beliefs of Official Islam. The foundation of Official Islam is that Islam is very difficult and very complex. This means that not only is the student unsure about what Islam is (since there is so much disagreement about it) but also they presume that such knowledge is impossible for anyone to obtain, except for imams and professors. We must establish that there is such a thing as sure and certain knowledge about Islam. Islam is a highly logical and coherent ideology. However, it uses a different logic system than ours. Once you see dualism, Islam becomes straightforward.

Official Islam preaches that if you don't believe its dogma, then you are vilified as a racist bigot. So the student has two fears—a secret fear of Islamic violence and a fear of being called a bigot.

We need to shape the situation and establish the point-of-view. You must shape the discussion and establish the common ground of critical thought and present the facts of the doctrine of Political Islam.

THE POINTS

Before we get into the actual shaping process, it is overwhelmingly important to confirm what the student says.

• Repeat what is said or restate the problem.

This step is valuable for several reasons. First, the other person has been heard and acknowledged. This is a powerful way to influence others—you have heard and understood them. Secondly, this may keep the person from repeating the same thing again and again.

There is another reason to repeat what is said. It gives you time to think about your response.

• Can we talk?

Acknowledge that Islam is not an easy subject to talk about, but can we talk? You want to hear what they have to say and see if some things you have learned lately could be enlightening.

Use your people skills to see if they are open and will allow discussion. It doesn't make much difference how much you know if they simply don't want to talk. Many supporters of Islam are not open to hearing any new information since their position is mostly build on some foundation of politically correct "tolerance".

The rest of these points are in no particular order:

• State that you are going to use critical thinking.

You will base your arguments on facts of the doctrine of Islam and not on what any imam or writer says. Point this out when their statements are not from Islamic doctrine. **Everything that Islam does is based upon its doctrine.** So what you say can be proven by the doctrine and history of Political Islam. Use facts, not opinions. Use the doctrine, not Muslims.

• Ask if they have any familiarity with the Koran or Mohammed?

This question is very powerful since it establishes a hierarchy of who knows what. If they have some familiarity with any of doctrine, now is a good time to find out how much they know and have read.

The next step is to explain how important knowing Koran and Mohammed is. Obviously, you have to have read some version of the Trilogy before you can do this step.

- Establish that the actions and words of Muslims are based upon the Trilogy.

There is sure and certain knowledge about Islam. Every Muslim agrees that there is no god but Allah and Mohammed is his prophet. The basis for Islamic knowledge comes from Allah (the Koran) and Mohammed (the Sunna, found in the Sira and the Hadith). If it is in the Trilogy, it is Islam. If it is not in the Trilogy, it is not Islam.

Mohammed is the supreme authority in Islam. No Muslim, no media pundit, no imam, no book, no article, not even the president of the US can be above Mohammed. Once you know Mohammed, you know the truth of Islam.

This is the heart of the matter. All Muslims are Mohammedans. (This does not mean that Muslims worship Mohammed. A Confucian does not worship Confucius, but lives his life according to the precepts of Confucius. In the same way, a Mohammedan patterns his life after Mohammed.)

Islam is simple. Islam is the political, religious and cultural doctrine found in the Trilogy.

After you understand this, your world changes. When you read an article in the *New York Times* by a government/university expert on Islam, you will see it has no merit until the conclusion of the experts is checked against the Sunna. If the "expert" agrees with Mohammed or Allah, then the conclusions are correct. If they violate the Sunna or the Koran, they are wrong.

What you will find, in nearly every case, is the article of the "expert" never contains the words "Mohammed" or "Allah". The "experts" may quote a single Koran verse, but never use Mohammed.

Think about this. There is only one Islam—the Sunna and the Koran. Why do we need the experts? No one needs a Muslim to define Islam. The Koran and Sunna do that for us. Once you know the doctrine, Islam is easy. You can grade the news reports, the government propaganda, the smart articles. You will see that none of the experts ever speak about the "why" of Islam. When you know the doctrine, you will always know why.

At this point the more sophisticated student will draw upon articles written by "moderate" Muslims. They say that reform is possible for Islam. And what will this new Islam be based upon? If the new reformed Islam is not based upon the Sunna and the Koran, then it is apostasy, the worst crime in Islam. There is no escape from the Koran and Sunna, ever.

The method is this: bring all arguments back to the Koran and the Sunna. If you are the expert, then bring in Koranic verses, but Koran specifics can be tricky. Stay with the Sunna (Mohammed) and you will never go wrong.

Once you introduce them to the idea of a true Islamic doctrine, you can go into a thousand directions to your chosen advantage. The doctrine is a devastating strategic weapon. The Sunna is also a weapon of magnificent power at small tactical details. Once you know Mohammed, there are unlimited stories to illustrate any point you want.

- Kafir-centric

There is no Islamic idea more important than that of the Kafir. Kafir transforms a theoretical Islam into a personal Islam.

Always point out to your student that they are a Kafir, just like you. Explain to them how that in Islam Kafirs are hated by Allah and how He plots against us. Kafirs can be enslaved, robbed, lied to, mocked, abused, tortured, raped and so on. There is no limit to the abuse that a Kafir can receive. On the other hand, a Kafir may be treated well, as that is Islam's dualistic nature.

What you see in Islam depends upon who you are. For example, when Mohammed executed the 800 male Jews in Medina, what is the judgment?

For the believers, it was a glorious day. Islam triumphed over the hated Jews. For the Kafirs it was a day of ethnic cleansing, a tragedy, and an end to free speech (the only crime the Jews had committed was that they denied that Mohammed was a prophet). The dhimmi (apologist) view is that we should not judge past times by our modern standards. Besides Christians have done a lot of bad things too.

Which was it? Triumph, tragedy or no discrimination? There is no answer, just different points-of-view. The dhimmi will always be sympathetic to Islam and the Muslim will be always be proud. But in debate, argument and teaching, be sure to tell the Kafir side of the story.

There is no way around this viewpoint problem, since Islam divides the world into believer, dhimmi and Kafir. What you want to do is to tell your side of the story. Don't argue with the Muslim or dhimmi point, just state that you have your point of view, that of the victim, the Kafir. You are not really arguing for anything but the inclusion of the rest of the story. You are showing what Islam is like for Kafirs, not Muslims. The other side of the story is the Muslim/dhimmi view. It is only fair to present the Kafir side of the story.

The concept of Kafir is what bonds you to the student. Both teacher and student have the common bond of being hated by Allah. Mohammed first used charm on Kafirs and then arguments. Finally, if the Kafirs actively resisted, he destroyed them.

- What is the basis for what the other person says? What is his authority?

This is an all-purpose question and the answer is usually an article in the media. Most people do not have the slightest idea where they get their Official Islam, so it is a good question to ask. There is no need to press, but there is a need for them to admit their lack of real knowledge, only opinion. It is also a good time to separate the person from their ideas by pointing out that they have been misled by people they trust.

It is always appropriate to ask if they have read the Koran, Sira and Hadith. If they say that they have read the Koran (a very rare event) then ask if they have read the entire Koran. If they have read the Koran, ask about their understanding abrogation. Do they know that all of the "good" verses are abrogated by the later verses?

Another question to ask is if they understand Islam from both Muslim and Kafir points of view? This Kafir view is an entirely new idea. Part of the Official Islam doctrine is that only the view is of Islam is true. Official Islam denies that there is such a thing as a Kafir view of Islam.

This seems like a lot to say, but you don't have to use that many words. Imagine that you find yourself in a discussion with a friend about Islam. You say to yourself that we are talking about Islam and it is time to shape the talk.

You might say, "Before we talk about Islam and women (or whatever point that is up for discussion) it is good to know that Islam becomes simple if you understand Mohammed. Instead of talking about an opinion of some 'expert', use the doctrine for just about every question in Islam. Once you know what Mohammed did or said, you can use fact-based logic about Islam.

You can say, "Do you understand that everything in Islam has two meanings? The Muslim viewpoint and the Kafir viewpoint? I only talk about Islam from the Kafir point-of-view."

Look at what you have set up in less than two minutes:

- Islam has a doctrine and Mohammed is necessary to understand it
- Most writing can be dismissed as opinion only
- Introduced an entirely new viewpoint, Kafir-centric reasoning
- Established that you are going to use critical thought, not opinions

In these few simple steps, you have put the discussion on an entirely different footing. The student's very ground of discussion has been destroyed.

All of those articles in the mainstream media by the Harvard professors and other Islamic scholars have been demoted to someone's personal opinion. More importantly, you have established that all truth of Islam is knowable and they don't know it. You have taken control of the discussion before the point is even discussed. You have shaped the debate.

- What does it mean if you are wrong?

This question goes to the heart of the problem. Most apologists are desperate to believe that Official Islam must be right, because if it is as they fear, then they will have to do something. To do something will mean that they will be socially ostracized by their friends.

The problem in using this technique is to remember to take the time to set up the situation. In boxing, you do not try to knock out the opponent with every blow. Most blows set up the situation for a real punch. In the same way, in a debate, you do not want to come out swinging. Take time to set up the punch.

With this shaping, you have also cut out the ground from under the other person's feet. You become the true multicultural person with this shaping. You are insisting that Islam be based upon its own doctrine, not some Western European basis. It may be politically incorrect to criticize a Muslim, but that rule does not apply to doctrine.

DUALISM

At some point it is always needed to introduce Islamic dualism. Dualism is covered in all of the CSPI Trilogy books. Islam does have many features that seem good on the surface. However, when you look further there is a contradicting idea, as well. It is the old Mecca-Medina concept again and again.

POLITICAL ISLAM IS 100% BAD FOR KAFIRS

People will dig up any fragment of good about Islam they can find. Part of a winning strategy is to deny that there is any good for Kafirs in Islam, none. If they can find one good fact or idea, then they will take refuge in it. Part of the shaping is to challenge the other person to show one good thing about Islam and then show that duality means something more powerful will offset the good point.

IN SUMMARY

Shape the debate or teaching moment by:

- Summarizing the opposition's point.
- Using critical thinking based on the doctrine of Islam, not the opinion of "experts" even if those experts are Muslims. Mohammed is the only expert.
- Proving your statements by using the doctrine and in particular, Mohammed. Show how the actions and words of all Muslims are based upon the Trilogy, their sole authority.
- Asking where they get their information.
- Presenting the Kafir viewpoint.

HOW TO USE THIS MATERIAL

This material must be practiced. You may not get it totally right the first time, but even one or two of these points will move the discussion to unfamiliar grounds—the truth of Islamic doctrine and history.

EXAMPLE CASES

Chapter 6

INTRODUCTION

The doctrine of Political Islam provides the strongest argument against Islam. The second strongest argument is the history of jihad.

In debating about Islam do not engage the others' arguments on their points. Instead create a new basis by bringing in facts from Islam's political nature, Kafirs, duality and submission.

Instead of resisting your opponents, use the principle of duality to show both sides of the contradiction. Point out that Islam always has two ways to treat the Kafirs and what you want to do is provide the rest of the doctrine that is left out of Official Islam. The apologists and Muslims present their viewpoint so all you want to do is to show the Kafir viewpoint.

All of the arguments found here are based on having read the Koran, Sira, and Hadith. You cannot argue about Islam, if you do not know Islamic doctrine.

FOUNDATIONAL

Your continual strategy is to stay with the Koran and Mohammed. When the other person brings up Christianity, stay with Islam If they want to talk about Christianity, say you will compare Jesus with Mohammed, but stay with Mohammed. If they want to talk about the Crusades, say they were in response to the jihad that conquered Christian lands. And jihad comes straight from the Islamic political doctrine.

If you will stay with the foundational doctrine, you will always prevail and persuade. The Koran and Mohammed are so negative that you can't lose.

Nearly every argument you hear is from the media and the media never talks about doctrine. So when you speak about doctrine, you are presenting new material. Your debate opponents have opinions; you have facts. Ask them where they got their arguments. You will be glad to tell them where you get your facts.

When they tell you about what their Muslim friend says, tell them that you have a Muslim friend called Mohammed. Your Muslim friend outranks their Muslim friend. If they get their information from some Muslim expert, the strategy does not change—go to Mohammed. He is the supreme expert; their expert is second rank, no matter who he is.

It is also a good time to ask if they have any Muslim apostate friends. This brings up the chance to introduce what apostasy means in the Hadith.

When they say that what Muslims do is in response to our failures, colonialism, foreign policy, whatever, show them how everything Muslims do is based upon the doctrine.

All of these case studies are based upon the doctrine of Islam.

CAN YOU READ ARABIC?

You may be asked if you can read Arabic. The implication is that Arabic is a unique language that can't be translated and therefore, how could you know what you are talking about? First, the Koran claims to be a universal message for all humanity for all times. If the message is universal, then it must be understood by all. If everybody cannot understand the message, then by definition it is not universal. So, which is it?

Another thing to consider is that over half of the Koran is about Kafirs and politics. Do you really think that a political message about a Kafir cannot be understood by the Kafir? If so, what is that message that cannot be understood?

Also, it must be made clear which Arabic is being spoken about. The Arabic of the Koran is classical Arabic which is about as similar to modern Arabic as the English of Chaucer is to modern English. Said in another way, not even a modern Arab can read classical Arabic. It is estimated that fewer than a thousand scholars who read classical Arabic can compose a paragraph in classical Arabic script on a random topic.

And what about the billion-plus Muslims who don't understand modern Arabic? If it is necessary to understand classical Arabic to understand what the Koran is about, then how can all those non-Arabic-speaking Muslims understand the Koran? And if they cannot understand the Koran, how can they be Muslims?

Ask the person who presents the argument if they have any opinions about the doctrine of Christianity. Then ask them if they read Hebrew, Aramaic or Biblical Greek? If they do not read those languages how can they form an opinion about something they have to read in translation?

Of course they can read it and form an opinion, the same way we can read and understand the Koran.

A secondary question is why would anyone want to believe that the Koran couldn't be understood? What is the purpose of believing that out of all the books in the world, it is the one that cannot be translated and understood?

The Koran is only 14% of the total doctrine[1] as found in the Koran, Sira and Hadith. Would the questioner believe that the other 86% of the doctrine, the Sira and Hadith, not be understood as well?

WELL, THE CHRISTIANS/JEWS DID...

There are two different ways to deal with comments about Christianity and Judaism.

Method A

Reject all conversation that is not about Islam. Reject all comparative religious talk. Insist on talking solely about Islam. If they want to talk about Christianity/Judaism fine, but don't respond, except to say that you want to talk about Islam, not comparative religion. When it is your turn, return to Islam. Refuse to engage in comparisons. Islam must be taken on its own. There is no comparison. Insist on discussing the Sunna and the Koran.

Method B

Ask if they have a reason that they don't want to talk about Islam, since they want to change the subject. The average person knows next to nothing about this subject and sometimes this gambit is merely a way to steer the conversation into a familiar ground.

They are just trying to prove that Islam is not any worse than Christianity. At this point, welcome the chance to compare the two, but choose the ground of comparison. The best place to start is with the founders. Compare Mohammed to Christ. The other good comparison is in ethics. Compare Islam's dualistic ethics to Christian unitary, Golden Rule ethics.

Another version of this argument is that the person will compare some failed Christian to a "good" Muslim they know at work. It is fairly useless to do personal comparisons. How do you choose which Muslim out of

---

1   http://cspipublishing.com/statistical/TrilogyStats/The_Relative_Sizes_of_the_Trilogy_Texts.html

1.5 billion Muslims and which Christian does you choose out of a couple billion Christians?

A variation on the "Well, the Christians did ..." is "What about the Crusades"? This is the time to say you welcome a comparison of the Crusades to jihad. Start with the question of why the Crusades were needed. Islamic jihad invaded the Christian Middle East and subjugated them. The Crusades were a response to a cry for help by the tortured and oppressed Christians in their native land. Did the Christians do some wrong things? Yes, but notice that the Crusades have been over nearly a thousand years. Jihad is active today. And while we are at it, why do academic libraries have many books on the Crusades, which lasted only 200 years, and so few on jihad, which has been going on for 1400 years? The West has analyzed the Crusades, *ad nauseam*, and has barely looked at jihad.

I KNOW THIS MUSLIM AND HE SAYS...

Why is the Muslim an expert on Islam? Remember, the average Muslim knows very little about the doctrine of Islam. Why? Because, historically the imams have acted as the high priests of Islam and they have never made the doctrine simple to understand. That is one way they keep their prestige and power.

It does not make any difference who the Muslim is. Once you know something about the doctrine of the Trilogy, you can say that you also know a Muslim, and his name is Mohammed, and what you say comes from the Sunna. In short, your Muslim, Mohammed, can trump your friend's Muslim on any issue of doctrine. If the Muslim your friend knows says something about Islam that agrees with Mohammed, then it is right. If what he says contradicts Mohammed, then he is wrong. Mohammed is the only Muslim who counts.

I KNOW THIS MUSLIM AND HE IS A NICE MAN

So a man is nice and he is a Muslim. What does that prove about Islam? He may follow the Golden Rule and not Islamic doctrine. That is, he may be a poor practitioner of Islam and a good person.

The first question to ask about "nice" Muslims is do they believe in the Koran and the Sunna of Mohammed? They will say yes. Now is the time to explain about the Islam of Mecca and the Islam of Medina. It is also time to explain about dualism and how Islam always has two faces.

Stay with the doctrine and the history of Islam, never get personal and talk about an individual Muslim. Actually, there is one way to talk about any Muslim, just show how what they do and say follows the doctrine.

MUSLIMS REJECTING SHARIA

You will discover that some Muslims say that they reject Sharia. What they mean is that they reject some parts of the Sharia. Since Sharia covers the details of the Five Pillars, including prayer, to reject all of the Sharia is to become an apostate.

The first question to ask any Muslim who rejects part of Sharia, is exactly what part they reject. Since the rules of Sharia are based upon the Sunna of Mohammed and the Koran, that means rejecting the Koran and the Sunna. But a Muslim must accept all of the Koran as the exact perfect manifestation of Allah. Therefore, the Sharia that is based on the Koran must be accepted as valid. In the same way, Mohammed is the perfect Muslim and is to be imitated in all matters. To reject Sharia based upon Sunna is to be an apostate.

Here is a summary of the proper Islamic attitude about Sharia:

> The word Sharia means "road," and the implied imagery of the term is that our life is like a road in a desert, with God the oasis we seek. Thus the primary focus of Sharia law is on humankind's journey toward intimacy with our Creator, and the Sharia's purpose is to establish the links or guideposts between God and humanity. The Sharia is the body of divine guidance, its structure, format, and construct. It is important to Muslims because it is the guide by which the Muslim determines what is good or ethical. To Muslim ears, "Sharia law" means all that is constitutional, ethical, right, and compassionate—the conditions necessary for what Americans call the pursuit of happiness. This is why many Muslims seek to base their national legal systems on Sharia law, for that is the highest authority they can claim on their behalf in correcting wrongs[2].

THAT IS NOT THE REAL ISLAM

When you bring up an atrocity by Islam—the 9/11 attacks, Beslan, Russia, Mumbai India—a common apologist response is that that is not the real Islam. Ask them how they know what is and is not "real" Islam. Real Islam comes from Mohammed and he frequently launched sneak attacks against Kafirs. For example, he attacked the Jews of Khaybar in a surprise raid in the

---

2 *What is Right with Islam*, Imam Feisal Rauf, Harper San Francisco, 2004, page 150.

morning (his favorite sneak attack time of day). After he had killed enough Jews so that the rest submitted, he then tortured some to find more buried treasure while his men raped many of the women. That is how Mohammed did atrocities, so murderous sneak attacks against civilian Kafirs is Sunna. If there is anyway that the event is similar to the Sunna, then it is the real Islam.

If you are quoting the Sharia, then it is the real Islam, by definition, as are the Koran and the Sunna.

THEY DON'T REALLY BELIEVE THAT

You reveal some horrific part of the doctrine and the other person says that Muslims don't really believe that. What do Muslims call themselves? The Believers. What do they believe? The Koran and the Sunna. They say that is what they believe. Now ask two questions: have you read and understood the Koran or the Sunna? If not, how do you know anything about what Muslims believe?

I KNOW THIS MUSLIM AND HE IS NOT VIOLENT

This is a restating of, "I know this Muslim and he is good man." He may be a non-practicing Muslim and a good man who follows the Golden Rule.

A non-violent Muslim believes in the Koran and the Sunna of Mohammed. The Koran suggests both violence and tolerance against the Kafirs. Today in America, the political power of Islam is just getting started, so Islam is still weak. When Mohammed was weak in Mecca, he did not kill anybody. Islam is still in the first phase of jihad here.

We know from the Sira that many Muslims just don't have the stomach for the violence. The Sira shows that Muslims can support jihad in many ways, besides personal violence. The "peaceful" Muslim you know is commanded to give money to Islamic charities and the charities give the money to the actual fighters.

WHAT ABOUT THE VIOLENCE IN THE OLD TESTAMENT?

Apologists love to bring up the violence in the Old Testament to show that Islam is no better or worse than Christianity and Judaism. This is another version of "I don't know anything about Islam so I will talk about what I do know—Christianity and Judaism."

There is only one way to prove or disprove the comparison: measure the differences in violence.

The first item is the definition of violence. The only violence that matters to someone outside either Islam or Judaism is what they do to the "other", or political violence. Cain killing Able is not political violence. Political violence is not killing a lamb for a meal or making an animal sacrifice. Note, however, both are violence for a vegan or a PETA member, but it is not violence against them.

We now need to compare the doctrines both quantitatively and qualitatively. The political violence of the Koran is called "fighting in Allah's cause", or jihad.

We must do more than measure the jihad in the Koran. Islam has three sacred texts: Koran, Sira and Hadith, the Islamic Trilogy. The Sira is Mohammed's biography. The Hadith are his traditions—what he did and said. Sira and Hadith form the Sunna.

It turns out that jihad occurs in large proportion in all three texts. Here is a chart about the results:

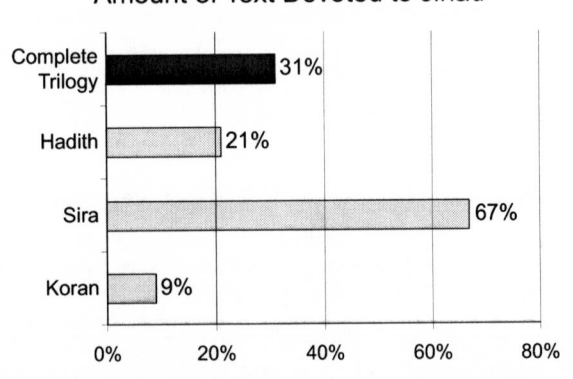

Basically, when Mohammed was a preacher of religion, Islam grew at the rate of 10 new Muslims per year. But when he turned to jihad, Islam grew at an average rate of 10,000 per year. All of the details of how to wage jihad are recorded in great detail. The Koran gives the great vision of jihad—world conquest by the political process. The Sira is a strategic manual and the Hadith is a tactical manual of jihad.

Now let's look at the Hebrew Bible. When all of the political violence is counted, we find that 5.6% of the text is devoted to political violence as opposed to 31% of the Islamic Trilogy.

When we count the magnitude of words devoted to political violence, we have 327,547 words in the Trilogy and 34,039 words in the Hebrew

Bible. The Trilogy has 9.6 times as much wordage devoted to political violence as the Hebrew Bible.

Words Devoted to Political Violence

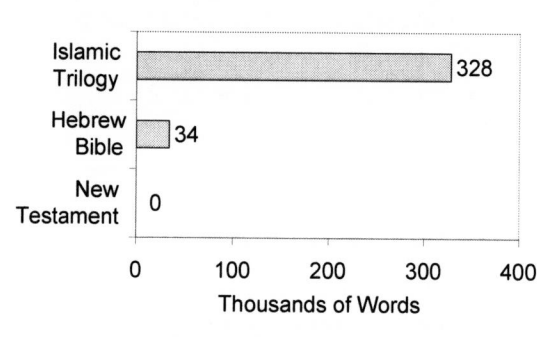

Thousands of Words

Then there is the qualitative measurement. The political violence of the Koran is eternal and universal. The political violence of the Bible is for that particular historical time and place.

Here is a measurement of the difference. Jihad has killed about 270 million non-Muslims over the last 1400 years. Jewish political violence killed 300,000 (an order of magnitude surmise) since the days of the Old Testament. As a comparison, jihad has killed thousands of times more people than Jewish political violence.

These figures are not about moderate Muslims or extremist Muslims. These figures are about the doctrine that Muslims say is perfect. All Muslims, without exception, believe in the perfect Koran and the perfect Sunna. Now, how much of it they are aware of is another question. But the doctrine is there for all of us to see and study.

The violence in the Trilogy is for all Muslims, in all places and for all time. Jihad is to stop only when every Kafir submits. Look at Mohammed, the perfect example. He was involved with violence until the day he died. And on his deathbed he directed violence against the Kafirs when he said in his last breath: "Let there be neither Christian or Jew left in Arabia."

IF ISLAM IS SO VIOLENT, HOW CAN IT BE SO SUCCESSFUL?

The Sira records that when Islam committed violence, it attracted new followers. As Osama bin Laden said: "People like a winning horse." After 9/11 in the US, new followers joined Islam. Communism was a political system that preached, promised and delivered violence and it attracted many people. Many people love violence. Have you noticed that in Hollywood violence is piled upon violence and people line up to pay money to see it.

THERE ARE DIFFERENT KINDS OF ISLAM

The differences in the various sects of Islam are due to religion, not politics. Take the Sunni/Shia split, its largest division. Both Sunnis and Shias completely agree on how to treat Kafirs and jihad. All Muslims subscribe to one of five schools of the Sharia and the Sharia's position regarding Kafirs and jihad is similar for all the sects.

The only big difference is when to use violent jihad or peaceful jihad against the Kafirs.

HADITH—SOME OF THOSE AREN'T REAL

If you quote a hadith to a Muslim and they don't like it, they will say, "Well, some of those hadiths are not acceptable (or not true or some other disclaimer)." Actually, when Muslims say this, they are practicing taqiyya, sacred deception and duality. If it is a hadith, then a Muslim cannot be denied the right to follow it. The Hadith are Sunna, the perfect example of Mohammed.

The hadiths cited in this book come from the very best collections—Al-Bukhari and Abu Muslim. These hadiths are the *creme de la creme* of hadiths and are called *sahih* (genuine) by top Islamic scholars. When Bukhari made his collection, he threw out 99% of those he found. Those 99% are the unsure ones, the other 1% that are used here are authoritative.

So the hadiths quoted here are genuine and real.

DOUBTS

Once you know something about the doctrine of Islam, you can wonder if you really know that much when you hear some Muslim (or apologist professor) say the following:

- The Koran forbids compulsion in religion [2:256]
- The Koran teaches the oneness of god and acceptance of all the prophets [2:285]
- Brotherhood [49:13]
- Acceptance of diversity [5:48]
- Peaceful relations with the Jews and Christians [3:64; 29:46; 5:5]
- Universal justice and fair dealings with all people [4:135; 5:8]

When you hear this good teaching from some Muslim or apologist you may doubt your knowledge. Maybe you have misjudged the doctrine and there is some way that Islam can be a force for the good of humanity.

Before we examine how good a force Islam is, let us examine how the doctrine is designed to deceive.

[Bukhari 4,52,267] *Mohammed said: war is deceit.*

Koran 4:142 *The hypocrites wish to deceive Allah, but He will deceive them.*

Koran 8:30 *Remember the unbelievers who plotted against you and sought to have you taken prisoner or to have you killed or banished. They made plans, as did Allah, but Allah is the best plotter of all.*

When it comes to deception, Mohammed was a deceiver and advised Muslims to deceive Kafirs. Allah plots against Kafirs and deceives them. All Muslims who follow the doctrine are deceivers of Kafirs. That is their sacred task. So when you hear about all of those good verses in the Koran, know that you are being deceived. All of the "good" verses in the Koran are denied later in the Koran. This is an example of the Mecca/Medina duality.

If Islam is so tolerant, why was there no Arab left to disagree with Mohammed at the time he died? When he re-entered Mecca as its conqueror, he issued death warrants for all those who had disagreed with him. Is this tolerance?

A supreme example of deception, taqiyya, is Imam Feisal Rauf's book *What's Right with Islam* in which he claims that the Constitution is based on Islamic principles and that Islam is based on the Golden Rule.

WHAT IS YOUR BASIS?

Instead of arguing against a point, ask the question: "Why do you say that? Where did you learn that?" In dealing with Islam, this is especially important as most people who speak about Islam with you get their information from a magazine, web or TV. Islam is a text based doctrine that is all about Mohammed. Tell them that you want to hear what Mohammed did and said. He is the basis to discuss Islam.

FILL IN THE BLANKS

It is a very useful technique to not oppose what your opponent/student says. Instead, give them the rest of the information. Fill in the other side of the duality. The beauty of this approach is that the other person is not being attacked at all, so they don't tend to push back and argue.

Islamic doctrine has two faces. When someone brings in some part about Islam that seems good, just give them the other side of the story. If they talk about Meccan Islam, give them the other half, the Medinan Islam.

TRANSITION

This is not scientific reasoning, but it is a debate strategy. When you are first beginning to debate in person, you may find yourself in unfamiliar areas and feel you lack knowledge about something. If you are debating online or writing a letter to the editor, then you can research the facts, but in person you may, for tactical purposes, decide to change the subject by making a transition. Muslims do this all the time by changing the subject with an accusation against the Crusades, Christians or colonialism.

You can win an argument by rhetorical tactics. This is not scientific reasoning, but emotional reasoning. It works so well that you should always be aware of it when it is used by others.

The technique is very simple—transition to Mohammed. It is always possible to move the discussion to Mohammed. For instance, if there is some talk about what is in the Koran, point out that the Koran repeatedly says that all Muslims must follow the perfect example of Mohammed. Once you get to Mohammed, you can move to abuse of women, hatred of Jews, violence against intellectuals and artists, slavery…

INSULTS

Don't ever attack the other person in any way. Don't raise your voice or insult. It never persuades and only makes the other person more angry and stubborn. All debate should be done from the angle of teaching and insults don't create a teaching moment. More than that, it shows you to be out of control and unprofessional.

If you are insulted, your response depends upon whether an apologist or a Muslim insults you. If a Muslim insults, thank them for being such a good Muslim and following the Koran and the Sunna. The Koran uses many insults and curses against Kafirs. Mohammed frequently cursed and insulted Kafirs. Insults are part of authoritarian reasoning and Islam. Thank them for showing how Islamic logic and reasoning work. Their next Islamic move should be to use some form of threat. Ask them if they want to display their threat by revealing it.

If they are not a Muslim, stay with the authoritarian thinking theme. Point out that insults, name-calling and put-downs are part of authoritarian thought. Attack the fact that authoritarian thought is part of Official Islam, the Big Lie.

SECULAR MUSLIMS DON'T BELIEVE THE RELIGIOUS "STUFF"

First, why talk about individual Muslims? What does any individual prove about any group? If you know of a Christian who cheats, does that prove anything about Christianity? No. Don't discuss Muslims, except to point out that they come in three flavors—Meccan, Medinan, and Golden Rule. A Golden Rule Muslim is actually a Kafir, since he follows Kafir ethics, not Islamic dualistic ethics.

If they are a secular Muslim, then what part of the Koran and the Sunna do they reject and why? Good luck on getting them to deny any part of it.

WHY SHOULDN'T MUSLIM WOMEN WEAR THE HIJAB?

The hijab is a symbol of Sharia compliance. The Sharia is based upon duality and submission. Hence, the hijab is a symbol of hatred, because it is a sign of support for Sharia law which includes the hatred of the Kafir and violence against them.

DEMANDING PRAYER AT WORK

Why should Kafirs submit to any Islamic demands? Freedom of religion does not mean the right to dictate what others do. Demanding to have special time for prayer is a political demand. If the Kafir does not allow it, then the Muslim does not have to pray. That is Islamic Sharia law, because the Sharia gives the rules for makeup prayers, when prayer is missed. While prayer is religious, the demand on the Kafir is a political demand.

ISLAMIC VIOLENCE IS CAUSED BY POVERTY AND OPPRESSION

This statement is the same as saying: "I do not have the slightest knowledge about the Sunna of Mohammed and am completely ignorant about the Koran of Medina."

During the last nine years of his life, Mohammed averaged a violent event every six weeks. He is the perfect Muslim who is the perfect model of behavior. Muslims are violent because Mohammed was violent. Violence is pure Sunna and does not need poverty or a manufactured oppression.

Besides, nearly every jihadist leader is from middle class and is well educated. They are far from poor or oppressed.

MODERATES CAN REFORM ISLAM FROM THE INSIDE.

Islam is the religious, political and cultural doctrine found in the Koran, Sira and Hadith. How does anyone reform any of the doctrine? Islam cannot change or be reformed according to its own doctrine. A Muslim can be reformed, but not Islam.

The Sira is comprised of 67% violence (jihad)[3]. Only 21% of the Hadith is about jihad. The Koran devotes 64% of its text to Kafirs[4] and every reference is bigoted, hateful and evil. How do you take this and reform it? No one can reform Islam.

The only reform a Muslim can offer is to not choose what is on the menu. This is what the so-called moderate Muslims do. The violence and hatred are in the doctrine, but they do not choose to accept it. But, they still defend Islam and deceive Kafirs about the true nature of Islam that they are avoiding. In other words, "moderate" Muslims are denying the true doctrine and deceiving us that it does not exist.

All moderates must be asked if they believe in the Koran and the Sunna of Mohammed. If they do then all the arguments in this section apply.

SHARIA LAW IS JUST LIKE JEWISH LAW.

Sharia law is based upon duality and submission. Sharia law expresses hatred for the Kafir and subjugates all women. Sharia law is designed for world conquest, subjugation, oppression and annihilation of all Kafir culture. Sharia law opposes our Constitution and says that it is to replace our form of government. Jewish law is about how to be a Jew and has no designs on non-Jews. Indeed, Jewish law states that the law of the land trumps Jewish law. Jewish law is not like Sharia law.

YOU ARE NOT A KAFIR; YOU ARE A PERSON OF THE BOOK

Muslims like to say this to Christians and Jews if they show knowledge about Kafirs. Kafirs believe that Mohammed was not a prophet. A person of the Book has to believe that Mohammed was the last of the prophets. A Christian has to believe that Jesus was not the Son of God, there is no

---

3   http://cspipublishing.com/statistical/TrilogyStats/Percentage_of_Trilogy_Text_Devoted_to_Jihad.html

4   http://cspipublishing.com/statistical/TrilogyStats/AmtTxtDevoted-Kafir.html

Holy Trinity, that the Gospels are in error, and that Jesus was not crucified. Only if you hold these beliefs, then you are a real Christian in the view of Islam. Since no Christian believes a doctrine which opposes the Gospels, a church going Christian is just Kafirs.

A Jew has to believe that the Torah is in error and that only the Koran has the only true stories about Moses, David, Abraham and the other Jewish patriarchs. If, additionally, the Jew accepts that Mohammed is the final prophet of the God of the Jews, then such a Jew is a person of the Book and a real Jew (according to Islam). Otherwise, the Jew is simply a Kafir.

TREAT THEM AS A FRIEND

The process of educating others about Political Islam can only start with someone who has agreed to discuss Islam. When we speak one-on-one, the only winning method is to talk as if you were talking to a friend. Never adopt a combative mode. Do not oppose and become emotional. Be a teacher. The dhimmi is a good person who is trying to do the right thing. They do not want to be a bigot and are terrified of being called a racist. They are filled with the media version of Official Islam. They went to school, even college, and they were taught the Official Islam and so it must be right.

Do not oppose them. Give them the added facts about the doctrine and relate everything from the Kafir point of view. For instance, what does it mean to Kafirs when a Muslim woman wears a burka or hijab? Teach them from the Sunna (as was done above); always give the story of Mohammed.

BRIDGE BUILDING AND INTERFAITH DIALOG

One of the most painful things is to watch ministers and rabbis go to interfaith dialogues with Muslims. The dhimmi religious leaders want to build a "bridge", but don't know the first thing about how a bridge is built. In the real world, when you build a bridge, you do survey work and learn about what both ends of the bridge will be built on. But the dhimmi bridge builders pride themselves on not knowing the first thing about the Muslim end of the bridge—not the first thing.

The dhimmis build one end for the bridge on their theology and ethics and the other end of the bridge is "tolerance", another word for saying that they will believe anything they are told by a Muslim. The bridges these religious dhimmi leaders build are based on fantasy. They are not building bridges, but are building rainbows. See how beautiful the illusion is? But, it is still an illusion.

A general condemnation of Christians, Jews, Hindus and Buddhists is that all the Kafir religions have reduced their doctrine to compassion and tolerance. That emotional quality is necessary, but it is also necessary to have knowledge and truth to go with it. Otherwise you wind up with idiot compassion. And that is what Christians, Jews, Hindus and Buddhists offer at interfaith dialogues—idiot compassion. They become useful idiots for Islam.

In debating with such dhimmis, praise their desire for peace, but point out their lack of knowledge. They are basically narcissists, who see the argument revolving around their own goodness, not truth. Point out how self-centered they are and how true compassion would include learning about Islam as well.

Show them how Islam has attempted to annihilate all Kafir religions for 1400 years. Show them that the peaceful periods of co-existence are merely temporary rests before annihilation. Make them dwell on suffering of Kafirs. Point out that Muslims never accept any responsibility for this suffering and deny it.

I HAVE SEEN MODERATE ISLAMIC WEB SITES

Someone surfs the web and finds a version of a kinder and gentler Islam. Why isn't that true? Isn't that hope?

The web site promises a tolerant and loving Islam, not like that terrible extremist Islam. This is the ultimate dream of all Kafirs. The dream is that moderate Muslims will forge a reformation. This dream ignores the simple fact that both the Wahabbis and the Taliban are reform movements that arose during the 20th century. They do not dilute the doctrine found in the Trilogy. They really walk Mohammed's talk.

So why is the Wahabbi the real Islam and the kinder/gentler Islam not possible? Islam means submission. Muslim means one who has submitted. Islam is the cause; Muslims are the effect. Islam makes Muslims; Muslims do not make Islam. What a Muslim says about Islam is immaterial. There is only one authority, Mohammed.

The kinder/gentler Islam is based upon the Islam preached in Mecca for 13 years. This Islam was followed by the violent jihad of Medina. Two different Mohammeds, two different Islams. So the answer to reform is to use the Meccan Koran and Meccan Islam.

There is a problem, however. Islam is a process; it is not static. Mecca is the beginning part of the process. You can't just throw it out. Then there is the matter of the Koran clearly stating that the later Islam of Medina is the stronger, better Islam. The Medinan Islam is the completion of Islam—you can't throw it out.

There is another problem. The Koran is perfect. The Sunna (Mohammed's sacred pattern of the perfect life) is sacred. How can you reject what is perfect? That would mean labeling Medina as bad and evil. Rejecting Medina would also mean rejecting the code that the Sharia is based upon.

We must end our ignorance and learn about the doctrine and history of Islam. It is no longer hard to do that. The entire corpus of Koran, Sira and Hadith can be held in one hand and has been made easy to read. It is immoral to be so ignorant. Turn to Mohammed, not some imam. Then you will get the whole truth and nothing but the truth.

RADICAL ISLAMIC GROUPS

What does "radical" mean? Does it mean killing, robbing, enslaving, assassination, torture, deception, jihad? As long as those behaviors occur with the Kafirs on the receiving end, they are all acts that were performed by Mohammed. If Mohammed performed these actions, then they are not radical. Mohammed defines normative behavior for all Muslims.

What happened in Mumbai, India, the World Trade Towers and Beslan, Russia was not radical. Each and every action at those sites was based upon the Sunna of Mohammed.

MODERATES ARE USING THE KORAN TO PROVE THE RADICALS TO BE WRONG

Anytime anyone references only the Koran when they are talking about Islam, you are dealing with a deceiver or an ignorant person. The Koran is only 16% of the Islamic canon. The Koran does not have enough in it to accomplish even one of Islam's vaunted Five Pillars. The Sira and the Hadith make up the 84% of Islamic canon that shows a Muslim how to be a Muslim.

The Hadith devotes 21% of its text to jihad[5]. The Sira devotes 67% of its words to jihad. Which "moderate" can deny those facts?

The Koran devotes 64% of its words to Kafirs, not Muslims. Out of all this material in the Koran, some of it in Mecca seems to promise goodness to the Kafir, but the later Koran takes away this chance of goodness.

---

5   http://cspipublishing.com/statistical/TrilogyStats/Percentage_of_Trilogy_Text_Devoted_to_Jihad.html

The "radicals," the Medinan Muslims, are right. The Meccan Muslims are deceivers, perhaps of themselves, but certainly deceivers without any doctrinal basis.

Disregard what anyone says, except Mohammed. Actually, there is one, and only one, Muslim who will give you the straight truth and that is an apostate, one who has left Islam.

DON'T MALIGN ISLAM'S HOLY PROPHET

Why is quoting from the Sira and Hadith maligning? Mohammed gave out the rules for rape in jihad. He owned sex slaves, told Muslims it was good to beat their wives, laughed when his enemy's head was thrown at his feet. It's in the book. Such behavior goes on for page after page, year after year. Why is referring to facts maligning?

THERE ARE FUNDAMENTALISTS IN EVERY RELIGION

We must be clear. All that matters is politics. Religion is prayer and Paradise and Judgment Day. These things don't concern us.

This statement assumes that Islam is comparable to other political systems and religions. What is remarkable is that this statement is only made by those who know nothing about the doctrine of Political Islam. They don't know Sunna from tuna. Mohammed is perfect. Every Muslim, without exception, is supposed to imitate Mohammed down to the slightest action. Is that fundamentalism? If so, then every Muslim is supposed to be a fundamentalist. It is the Sunna.

INTERFAITH DIALOGUE WILL LET US MEET MUSLIMS AND CHANGE THEM

So you change some Muslims, so what? Are you going to change Islam? No. Is a Muslim going to change Islam? No. Islam is found in the Koran, Sira and Hadith. That is not going to change.

You can reform a Muslim and make them an apostate, but you cannot reform Islam.

THE KORAN HAS LOTS OF PEACEFUL VERSES

What does that prove? There have been men who killed a wife in jealousy. The fact that the great majority of his life was good does nothing about his being guilty of murder for only a second.

Mein Kampf is only 7% Jew-hatred. That means that it is 93% good and therefore, *Mein Kampf* is a good book. Ridiculous.

NOT ALL MUSLIMS WILL DECEIVE YOU

No, and for many different reasons. But deceiving the Kafir about Islam is ethical. So why do you want to do business with someone who has a sacred directive to lie when it helps Islam?

Every Muslim has three natures—Meccan Islam, Medinan Islam and Kafir. If he is manifesting his Kafir nature and the Golden Rule, then he is honest. So honesty is proof of his Kafir nature, not his Islamic nature.

IT ALL DEPENDS ON HOW YOU INTERPRET IT

There is truth to the fact that there are many things in the Koran that depend upon interpretation. As an example, Muslims are to command good and forbid wrong. This comes from a verse in the Koran. Interpretation goes into exactly who does this and how they are to do it. But this is a religious matter.

However, the way that Kafirs are to be treated is not in this category. It is true that the Koran says two different things about how to treat Kafirs. There is both tolerance and jihad. But this is not a matter of interpretation. The tolerance is advised when Islam is weak, jihad comes when it is strong.

The interpretation argument is an attempt to deal with duality in the Koran. Usually, the interpretation argument is related to saying that there are good and bad verses in the Bible. Today Jews don't use those violent verses to blow people up; they don't interpret it that way. So, if Muslims would just interpret the Koran in the right way, we could all get along.

But Muslims do interpret the Koran the right way according to Mohammed. The Koran is a dualistic document and that is what Muslims do. Some of them are playing good cop and a few play bad cop. Dualism reigns and the dhimmis pretend that the good cops will interpret the Koran the right way and change the minds of the bad cops. Not! The proper interpretation of Islam is that the bad cops outrank the good cops.

Another approach to interpretation is the Sharia. Sharia is the classical interpretation of Koran and Sunna by the finest Islamic scholars. As an example the Sharia says that jihad is killing Kafirs, not internal struggle. That is the proper interpretation of the Koran.

All of these arguments amount to the same thing—use the doctrine of Political Islam to provide a complete picture of Islam.

REFUTING OFFICIAL ISLAM

Chapter 7

INTRODUCTION

Each and every point of Official Islam is at best a half-truth. Since many people believe these half-truths, it is very important to know how to refute the errors of Official Islam.

Here is a point by point refutation:

- The religion of Islam is similar to Christianity and Judaism. They all worship the same god.

Islam is not only a religion, however, but a complete civilization with a political system of Sharia law and an Arab culture. It is the politics of Islam that are ruinous, not the religion. The Koran has 64% of its text devoted to the politics of the Kafir, not how to be a Muslim. The Sira (Mohammed's biography) devotes 67% of its words to jihad. Religion plays very little part in the Sira. Mohammed was a failure until he turned to politics and jihad. Islam's success depends upon its politics, even today.

The religion of Islam is the Teflon cloak of Political Islam. People do not think of Islam as a political system, but a religion. You cannot criticize religion, so you cannot criticize Islam. This gets Political Islam off the hook.

Both Christianity and Judaism have the Golden Rule as their central ethical principle. Islam does not have a Golden Rule, but instead has dualistic ethics with one set of rules for Muslims and another set for Kafirs. The Koran repeatedly says that the scriptures of the Jews and Christians are corrupt and filled with errors.

The Koran defines Allah. The Hebrew Bible defines the Jewish god. Allah condemns, rails against and curses the Jews, but the god of the Hebrew Bible loves the Jews.

The Christian god is defined by the New Testament and loves humanity. Allah does not love humanity, but hates the Kafirs (non-Muslims) and only loves Muslims. The Koran insists that Jesus was not divine, was not crucified and was not resurrected. The Koran says that the Christian Trinity is God,

42

Mary and Jesus and then adds that there is no Trinity. The Koran rejects every principle of Christianity.

The Jesus of the Koran is called Isa. Isa is not Jesus. And in the same way, the Musa of the Koran is not the Moses of the Torah. Every single "prophet" of the Koran that has a Jewish name is not actually the same prophet of the Torah.

The concept of the commonality of Abrahamic faiths is purely an Islamic assertion, without evidence.

Judaism and Christianity share the Hebrew Bible as being valid scripture. Islam denies the validity of the Hebrew Bible.

• Good Muslims prove that Islam is good

Muslims *per se* prove nothing about Islam. Islam is the doctrine found in the Koran, Sira and Hadith. There is absolutely nothing that any Muslim can do about the doctrine of Islam, except to choose what part of it to follow. The word Islam means submission; the word Muslim refers to one who submits. This establishes cause and effect—Islam causes Muslims; Muslims do not cause Islam.

Besides, what is a "good" Muslim? Kafirs mean that a good Muslim is someone who seems nice. But that is a subjective and personal standard. The only measure of "goodness" of a Muslim is the Islamic doctrine. A good Muslim follows the Koran and the Sunna. So even if the Muslim seems nice that proves not a single thing about the Koran, Sira and Hadith.

It is faulty thinking to believe that everything that a Muslim does is pure Islam. Those who call themselves Muslims are also attracted to Kafir civilization. Few Muslims follow pure Islam. Muslims are also part Kafir and the goodness is due to their Kafir nature, not their Islamic nature. When Muslims are good to Kafirs they are following the Golden Rule, a Christian, Jewish, Buddhist, Hindu and atheist ethic, not Islamic ethical dualism which asserts Muslims should not take Kafirs as friends.

• There are no jihadists, just extremists

This naming is either pure dhimmitude or deceit. It is impossible to be an extremist if you are following the Sunna of Mohammed. Islam rose to power through continued violence for nine straight years with an act of violence, on the average, every six weeks. The act of jihad is not extremism, but a manifestation of the core political doctrine of Islam. Put another way, none of the jihadists on 9/11 were extremists, but were extraordinary Muslims who followed the Sunna of Mohammed.

- Islam must be accommodated in as many ways as possible

This is dhimmitude (serving the needs of Islam) based upon ignorance and fear. Any student of Islamic history can show that Islam is never accommodated until the host culture follows Sharia. Mohammed was not satisfied until every person in Arabia submitted to Islam.

Accommodation of Islam means the end of free speech, free thought, freedom of religion, freedom of the press and our civilization.

- One of the proofs of Islam's greatness that Muslims offer is the Islamic Golden Age, humanity's best days.

The Golden Age is discussed in full in Chapter 8.

- Violence by Muslims is due to their being poor and oppressed

This explanation works best if you are a Marxist of some flavor who believes that economics and materialism is the driver for human behavior. Anyone who has studied Islamic doctrine and history knows that Islam is based upon violence and that without violence Mohammed would have died a failure. Jihad was his best invention and was the reason for his success in Medina. In Mecca he tried religion as a basis for success and failed.

Violence by Muslims against Kafirs is mandated by pure Islamic doctrine.

- The West got the basis of its intellectual world from Islam

When Islam destroyed the Greek culture of Anatolia and the Mediterranean, many of the surviving Greek and Roman texts were translated by Arabic Christians into Arabic. Later when Europe began to recover from the destruction of the Roman Empire by barbarians and the destruction of the Byzantine Empire by Islam, the Arabic translations became part of the recovery process as the old texts were translated back into European languages.

So as a result of the destruction of Greek culture and the preservation of the texts by Christian Arabs, Islam gets credit for saving European culture. Imagine that you had a valuable art collection that was stolen. Then the thieves burned your house. Afterwards, the police recovered your stolen art. Should the thieves get credit for the preservation of your art?

- The Crusades were a great evil

The Christians of Europe committed some grievous errors in the Crusades. The worst mistake was attacking Constantinople and fatally weakening the Greek Byzantine Empire. This attack led to Islam's success in conquering the Greek Byzantines, one of humanity's great tragedies.

Another dreadful error was the killing of thousands of Jews on the way to Jerusalem. Persecution of Jews occurred on more than one Crusade.

Having said that, it was one of the few times that European Christians came to the aid of their tortured Orthodox Christian brothers. Remember—the Crusades were defensive warfare. Islam invaded and conquered the Christians of the Middle East. When the Orthodox Christians cried out for help, the European Christians responded. Since that time, most Christians have steadfastly ignored the suffering of their Orthodox brothers.

- There are moderate Muslims and a few extremist Muslims

This is a perfect example of making statements about Islam based upon the Golden Rule and ignorance (or deceit) of the doctrine and history of Islam.

The only scale for measuring Muslims is Islam, not our ethics. Only the Koran and the Sunna give us the scale to measure a Muslim. Any Muslim that follows the doctrine of either Meccan Islam or Medinan Islam is a moderate. Medinan Muslims (jihadists) are moderates, just like Meccan Muslims are moderates.

The only extremist Muslim is an apostate, since apostasy is the "extreme" in Islam that is condemned.

- Islam is found in the Koran (Mohammed is never discussed)

This is the grand error of Official Islam. Once you know Mohammed, you know Islam. Once you know Mohammed, you know you are a Kafir and it is the purpose of Islam to annihilate you and your culture.

Therefore, it is the prime directive of Official Islam to never mention Mohammed and only talk about the Koran, the book everybody has heard of and nobody has read (and is considered impossible to understand). Sheer belief in the profound nature of the Koran is superstitious behavior.

If someone tries to explain Islam based upon the Koran, he knows very little about this subject. Immediately shift the conversation to Mohammed. You can't defeat Islam using the Koran, unless you are very skillful, but anyone can use Mohammed and make major ideological points easily.

Of the three Islamic texts—Koran, Sira and Hadith—the Koran is about 16% of the total content of the doctrine[1]. Islam is 84% Mohammed and 16% Koran. To know Islam, know Mohammed.

Notice the brilliance of moving the Kafirs' attention to the Koran, not the Sunna. The conventional wisdom is that you have to understand the Koran to understand Islam. That is what our generation has been taught in our schools. It used to be that the word Islam was not used, but instead the word was Mohammedanism. That name points to truth and to Mohammed. But everybody looks to the book they cannot understand, the Koran.

The Koran has been made impossible to understand without Mohammed. Most of the educated Kafirs never think about Mohammed, they are left ignorant and believing whatever Muslims say.

• The "bad stuff" in the Koran is just how it is interpreted

Luckily all of the bad stuff in the Koran has been interpreted in the Sharia, so we don't need to worry about interpretation. The Sharia says that the verses about fighting in Allah's cause means killing Kafirs.

There is no "bad stuff" in the Koran. The Koran is crystal clear in its nature. The fact that violence is repeatedly preached in the Koran does not make the Koran bad. Everything is the Koran is pure Islamic goodness. Jihad is part of that Islamic goodness.

Indeed, the entire concept of "good" and "bad" is un-Islamic. In contrast, Islam is based upon what is permitted and not permitted.

• Good Muslims will reform the "extremists"

As long as they are following the Sunna, a Muslim is a "good" Muslim. But extremists are merely Medinan Muslims, since they follow the Medinan doctrine of jihad. Extremists are jihadists. Jihadists are the best Muslims and don't need reform. Indeed, the Koran gives the jihadists political power over the Meccan Muslims, the ones we call good Muslims. Meccan Muslims are subordinate to Medinan Muslims, so reform can only come from Medinan Muslims, not the Meccan Muslims.

• Islam is the religion of tolerance

This is Sunna: when Mohammed became a prophet of Allah there were 360 religions in Mecca that were practiced at the Kabah. The Arabs were a very tolerant people. There had never been a religious war in Arabia until Mohammed.

---

1   http://cspipublishing.com/statistical/TrilogyStats/The_Relative_Sizes_of_the_Trilogy_Texts.html

After Mohammed came torture, murder, assassinations, enslavement, rape, theft and deceit. After 23 years of Mohammed, there were no other religions tolerated in Arabia. Mohammed was absolutely intolerant of all Kafirs. Mohammed was one of the most intolerant men who ever lived; therefore, Islam is one of the most intolerant political systems in history.

• Islam has a Golden Rule

Show me the Islamic Golden Rule. It is not found in the Koran, the Sira or the Hadith. The very concept of "Kafir" means that the Golden Rule cannot exist. There is no Golden Rule in Islam, since it divides humanity into two unequal groups—believer and Kafir.

After Mohammed became a prophet of Allah, he attacked everyone who did not agree with him. He kept attacking, first verbally and then physically, until everyone agreed to do exactly what he said. That is not the Golden Rule, but it is the Sunna. Mohammed did not follow the Golden Rule, therefore, it is not Sunna, and it is not Islam.

• Islam is a wonderful part of American culture

American culture is founded on the moral principle of the Golden Rule and the intellectual principle of critical thought. The Golden Rule is manifest in our Declaration of Independence and the Constitution. We have full legal equality of sex, race, religion and freedom of thought, ideas and the media.

Islam denies all of these principles with its dualistic ethics and dualistic logic. It is Islam's desire to eliminate all of our civilization and it is not part of it, whatsoever. It is not possible for Islam to be a part of our civilization, since it denies our core values.

• Islam is the religion of freedom

This is an insult to Islam, since it is the civilization of slaves. Mohammed was a slave of Allah. Muslims are the slaves of Allah. Mohammed enslaved those who did not agree with what he said. Every Muslim is a slave to the Sharia. Freedom is an anathema in Islam.

To leave Islam is a death sentence. Apostasy is the worst crime in Islam. If you cannot leave Islam, how is it free?

GOLDEN AGE?

Chapter 8

INTRODUCTION

It is important to understand the true Islamic Golden Age as it is such a popular argument about the greatness of the intellectual power of Islam. The Golden Age is part of Official Islam and is *taqiyya* (deception).

The Islamic Golden Age occured in two places—Moorish Spain and Baghdad in the ninth and tenth century. The oft-told Big Lie goes like this: Islam established a paradise on earth where Christians, Jews and Muslims lived in peace. Everybody got along. People were wealthy and knowledge flowed from the Islamic scholars in an unprecedented wave. While Europe was in the Dark Ages, Islam was a light unto the world. The only way that Europeans moved out of the Dark Ages was through the charity of Islamic knowledge.

That is the short version told by our dhimmi professors in such works as *The Oxford History of Islam*. Let us examine the Islamic Golden Age.

First things, first. Islam invaded Baghdad and Spain with the sword in hand. Islam killed so many people that the remainder surrendered. Those who surrendered and did not convert were raped, robbed and made dhimmis, except for those who were made slaves and shipped to another part of the Islamic empire. How Golden a beginning is that?

The Muslim masters were the new rulers who put Sharia law in place. What was the level of culture of the Muslims when they set up Baghdad as the imperial city? Islam was only a century away from Mohammed. There had never been a book written in Arabic until the Koran. Architecture consisted of mud huts. Arabia was barely out of the bronze age. Superstition ruled and the "science" of Mohammed as shown in the Hadith:

- The first men were 90 feet tall.
- One wing of a fly carries a disease, but the other wing is a cure for the disease.
- Black cumin will cure all diseases except death.
- Indian incense will cure seven diseases.

48

- Honey will cure diarrhea.
- A fever is caused by the heat from Hell.
- The sun sets at night beneath the throne of Allah.

This was the state of Islamic knowledge when Islam conquered Baghdad in the Christian nation of what is now Iraq. In short, Islam brought nothing to the intellectual table to start the Golden Age. The knowledge of the Golden Age in Baghdad came from the conquered Jews, Christians, Persians, and Hindus.

Islam took the "Arabic" numerals and the zero from the Hindus. The parabolic arch came from Assyria, the dome from Persia, and the barrel vault came from the Romans. Suddenly, the ignorant jihadists "owned" the world's finest minds. This explains how so much of the Islamic knowledge was actually translated into Arabic by Christians. O'Leary's book *How Greek Science Passed to the Arabs* gives a list of the best known scholars of the Baghdad (Abbasid caliphate) Golden Age. Out of theses 22 "Muslim" scholars, 20 were Christian, 1 was Persian and 1 was Muslim. Each and everyone had an Arabic name, so it is assumed that they were Muslim. It was the Christians Assyrians who translated the Greek philosophers into Syriac and then Arabic. It had to be this way. The Christians had a long tradition of education and learning that came from the Greeks, Jews and Romans; the Muslims had none. It had to be Christian Kafirs who brought the Greek and Roman knowledge to the Muslims. Ironically, the Muslims claim all of the credit for the translations saving Greek knowledge from the Dark Ages (more about that name later).

Another example of taking credit is found in Iraqi history texts which claim that the Assyrians, Sumerians, and Babylonians were all Arabs. This allows Islam to take credit for earlier work.

Islam makes great claims for its advanced medicine, which was the best in the West. However, the Christians and Jews were the chief practitioners. For 200 years the Bakhtishu family, Assyrian Christians, were the physicians to the Caliphs of Baghdad.

The Baghdad Golden Age disappeared as the persecution of the Christian dhimmis continued, and they converted to Islam. Once the pool of Kafir talent became Muslims the gold went out of the Golden Age.

The Golden Age of Spain is much the same. Let's examine the perfect society of Christian, Jew and Muslim living in such harmony. Moorish Spain is portrayed as the high point of multi-cultural existence and the perfect expression of Islamic society. Islam came to Spain by the sword. That invasion started an 800-year war with the Christians fighting against the constant Islamic invasion at the border between Spain and Europe.

Why does a struggle of 800 years not sound so Golden? If Islamic Spain was such a Golden Age, then why did the Spanish die in furious battles to throw out the Muslims? Why is Islamic imperialism painted as such a beautiful thing?

At this point it may seem as if there were no Islamic intellectual work that was of any value. This is not true, but the Golden Age propaganda is so strong, that a case must be established that the Golden Age was not what is portrayed—a proof of Islam's wonderful multicultural paradise and superior intellectual achievements.

But even the Muslim scholars had to contend with an intellectual world that was limited by the Koran and the Sunna. No thoughts were allowed that went beyond these small and strict bounds. Averroes was one of the best-known scholars of Moorish Spain and was very influential with both Christians and Jews. His writings were not Islamic enough and he was banished until shortly before his death. Many of his writings were burned. No Islamic school of thought followed him. Only Europeans honored his intelligence.

Al Farabi was a Muslim thinker of the first rank and used Greek reasoning to conclude that logical thought was superior to revelation, an Islamic heresy. He used critical thought examining the Koran and rejected predestination. He illustrates the idea that the best Muslim scholars were part Kafir.

Al Khwarzimi was an Islamic scholar in mathematics and astronomy. His translated works introduced Hindu mathematics to Kafirs. His work was the basis of algebra and the algorithm.

Even during the Golden Age, the Muslim scholarly output was small and depended upon Kafirs. In the modern world, Muslims have never won a single Nobel Prize in science, medicine or chemistry by themselves. There have been 8 prizes won by Muslims who worked with Kafirs in Kafir countries. But there has never been a Noble Prize for Muslim research in a Muslim nation.

Yes, there are Muslim thinkers who can produce good intellectual work, but they are outstanding individuals and are not typical. Saudi Arabia is the purest Islamic country and has untold billions to support any project they choose. In 2003 there were only 171 patents granted to Saudis[1]; compare this with 16,328 patents by South Korea[2]. Why is this?

---

1   *Arab Human Development Report 2003: Building a Knowledge Society*, UN Publications, 2003, pg. 11.

2   ibid

This is not a modern phenomenon. It goes back 1400 years. The only explanation lies with the nature of Islam itself and its limits on freedom of expression, education, human rights, etc.

There is one more thing to notice about what Islam produced with the Kafir knowledge. Some of their best work was in math, but it never went anywhere practically. Al Khwarzimi may have developed the algorithm, but it was Kafirs who put it to use in computers. Algebra was only an idea in a book. It was a Kafir, Sir Isaac Newton, who used algebra to develop calculus and differential equations. And with calculus and differential equations, Newton was able to show how the planets moved in orbit. Muslims used glass for windows in their mosques, while Kafirs used it in telescopes and microscopes.

THE FINAL WORD

The basic problem with the Golden Age is the status of the Kafirs. They were dhimmis, third class citizens without civil rights.

The Islamic ethical basis of the Golden Age was dualism—one set of ethics for Muslims and another set for Kafirs. Kafirs had to wear special clothing, were prohibited from being in positions of power, had to get permission to repair their houses of worship and could not testify in courts against a Muslim. If a Kafir killed a Muslim, he received a death sentence, but if a Muslim killed a Kafir, he paid a fine. A Kafir was inferior in every way to a Muslim. How Golden is that?

Every Kafir lived under Sharia law and Sharia law is based upon the evil of the principles of submission and duality. Sharia is oppressive and cruel.

Where did all this propaganda about the Golden Age come from? Two sets of people created the Golden Age myth—French intellectuals such as Gibbons, Voltaire, and Jewish writers such as Graetz. Both had the same motivation—hatred of the Catholic church. Building up the wonderful Islamic culture was a reaction to the hated Catholics. There were Kafirs who prospered under Islam. They submitted and served Islam and their masters rewarded them. Every occupying army can persuade some locals to act as traitors for their own personal gain. Some of these Kafirs had positions of some power, but in the end, they were still servants of Islam.

A CASE STUDY

Chapter 9

AN EXAMPLE

Here is a typical comment from a religious leader in response to a letter in a paper that was critical of Islam:

> We find otherwise good people become bigots when they discuss Islam. They judge Islam by its extremists. Unfortunately, Islamophobia is the last remaining acceptable prejudice.
>
> When they say that Islam abuses women, murders apostates and hates outsiders, they are talking about a counterfeit Islam. We find such hatred amongst both Jews and Christians as well.
>
> One Muslim writer pointed out that there is enough in the Koran for global holy war. But there is also enough there for people of a peaceful mind-set to discover a path to enlightenment and peace. There is bad material in the Hebrew Scriptures and the New Testament as well. But we can also find sublime uplifting passages.
>
> Our spiritual work, as brothers of the Abrahamic faith, is to combat ugly anti-Muslim sentiments and make it socially intolerable.
>
> Signed: Rabbi ...

THE RESPONSE

Let us start with an analysis of content. Here are some major points:

- There is not one mention of Mohammed or Allah (Koran)
- Bigots judge Islam by its extremists (what is an extremist? No scale to measure extremism is given)
- Being critical of Islam is prejudiced
- Denies that Islam abuses women, murders apostates and hates outsiders
- What is the basis for determining a counterfeit Islam? (If something is false, how do we determine what is true or false. We must have a standard.)

- Who is the "one Muslim writer"?
- There are good verses and bad verses in the Koran, but there is good stuff and bad stuff in the Bible
- Jews, Christians and Muslims are part of the same Abrahamic faith
- In the last paragraph we are now hating people (not Islam)
- People who speak against Islam must be condemned in society
- Who is this man to make such moral judgments?

There are many points to attack. Here is one reply that tackles most of these points. Notice that even though the writer is a rabbi, it makes no difference; he could be a Christian or any other dhimmi.

First things first. There is not one single fact about Islam in the entire letter. We know this because anything that relates to the doctrine of Islam includes the words Allah or Mohammed. Instead of facts, the writer substitutes his authoritarian reasoning and the opinion of "one Muslim writer", not Mohammed. He declares from his high moral ground the judgment that anyone who criticizes Islam is a bigot. Why? He decrees it. Evidence? Facts? No need for those when you have the authority to make decrees.

- they are talking about a counterfeit Islam.

He uses the word "counterfeit". And what is the standard to determine counterfeit from the real deal? Simple, the one and only standard of Islam is the Koran and the Sunna. Let's use that standard.

- When they say that Islam abuses women

For those who enjoy fact-based logic: Does Islam abuse women? Let's start with the Koran:

> Koran 4:34 *Allah has made men superior to women because men spend their wealth to support them. Therefore, virtuous women are obedient, and they are to guard their unseen parts as Allah has guarded them. As for women whom you fear will rebel, admonish them first, and then send them to a separate bed, and then beat them. But if they are obedient after that, then do nothing further; surely Allah is exalted and great!*

Now let us turn to Mohammed as found in the Hadith (Mohammed's traditions). Mohammed's words and actions (Sunna) are half of Islam. If Mohammed did it, then it not extremist.

> Abu Dawud 11, 2142 *Mohammed said: A man will not be asked as to why he beat his wife.*

This hadith equates camels, slaves and women.

> Abu Dawud 11, 2155 *Mohammed said: If one of you marries a woman or buys a slave, he should say: "O Allah, I ask You for the good in her, and in the disposition You have given her; I take refuge in You from the evil in her, and in the disposition You have given her." When he buys a camel, he should take hold of the top of its hump and say the same kind of thing.*

Here is more advice about slaves and women:

> Bukhari 7,62,132 *The Prophet said, "None of you should flog his wife as he flogs a slave and then have sexual intercourse with her in the last part of the day."*

A statistical summary is revealing. Below is a table that summarizes all of the hadiths about women that can be found in the Hadith by Bukhari. Each hadith was judged as to whether the woman was superior to men, equal to men or inferior. All of the superior hadiths were about women as mothers. The equality sentences were about being judged equally on Judgment Day. And what is one of the things a woman is judged on? How well she pleased her husband. The conclusion is that Islamic doctrine debases women.

	Superior	Inferior	Equal	Neutral
Number hadiths	7	8	157	47
Percentage of text	0,6 %	89 %	10 %	Not included

Equality of Sexes in Hadith

- murders apostates

Does Islam murder apostates (those who leave Islam)? Let us look at what the Sunna of Mohammed says:

> Bukhari 9, 83, 37 *[...] This news reached Allah's Apostle , so he sent (men) to follow their traces and they were captured and brought (to the Prophet). He then ordered to cut their hands and feet, and their eyes were branded with heated pieces of iron, and then he threw them in the sun till they died." I said, "What can be worse than what those people did? They deserted Islam, committed murder and theft."*

> Bukhari 9, 84, 57 *[...] I would have killed them according to the statement of Allah's Apostle, 'Whoever changed his Islamic religion, then kill him.'"*

Bukhari 9, 84, 58 [...] Behold: There was a fettered man beside Abu Muisa. Mu'adh asked, "Who is this (man)?" Abu Muisa said, "He was a Jew and became a Muslim and then reverted back to Judaism." Then Abu Muisa requested Mu'adh to sit down but Mu'adh said, "I will not sit down till he has been killed. This is the judgment of Allah and His Apostle (for such cases) and repeated it thrice. Then Abu Musa ordered that the man be killed, and he was killed. [...]

It is Sunna to kill apostates, so Islamic doctrine says to kill apostates. As an aside, when Mohammed died, the next caliph, Abu Bakr, killed apostates for two years because many Muslims wanted to quit. Abu Bakr persuaded the survivors to be contented Muslims.

• hates outsiders

Does Islam hate outsiders? Let us turn to the Koran and consider a word introduced and defined by the Koran. The word is Kafir (unbeliever), the ultimate outsider. More that half of the Koran is about Kafirs. The only good verses about Kafirs are abrogated later in the Koran. Allah hates Kafirs and plots against them.

Koran 40:35 They who dispute the signs of Allah [Kafirs] without authority having reached them are greatly hated by Allah and the believers. So Allah seals up every arrogant, disdainful heart.

Koran 86:15 They plot and scheme against you [Mohammed], and I plot and scheme against them. Therefore, deal calmly with the Kafirs and leave them alone for a while.

Kafirs can be tortured, mocked, robbed, enslaved and raped. The Kafir argument may be carried further with more details. Make a list of what Mohammed did to all of his Kafir neighbors. In every case he attacked them when they would not submit to his demands.

The rabbi grapples with the duality of the Koran in his paragraph about the good and the bad in the Koran. He makes the usual argument: "it all depends on the interpretation." This drive for interpretation is an attempt to eliminate the contradictory nature of the Koran. The Koran is filled with contradictions at all levels, and this was pointed out to Mohammed by the Meccans of his day. The Koran uses the principle of abrogation to resolve these contradictions. The later verse is better than the earlier verse.

But since everything in the Koran is the exact word of Allah and Allah is perfect and cannot lie, then every verse of the Koran is true, even if it is contradictory. This violates our logic so we try to decide which side is the truth. But both sides are true in dualistic logic. The Koran is a dualistic document and Islam is a dualistic ideology. The answer to the question: "which side is it?" is always all of the above. That is the genius of Islam—it can have it both ways, and this confuses the Kafirs.

- as brothers of the Abrahamic faith

Now to the idea of: "brothers in the Abrahamic faith." Let us look to Mohammed for the relationship between Muslims and their Jewish brothers. At first, Mohammed proved his validity by the fact that his angel was Gabriel, the angel of the prophets of the Jews. Therefore, he was of the same prophetic linage. Since there were no Jews in Mecca to deny him, the idea worked.

When he went to Medina, which was half Jewish, the rabbis told him he was no prophet in the lineage of the Jews. No one could contradict Mohammed and as a result, three years later, there was not a single Jew left in Medina. They were annihilated. Then he attacked the Jews of Khaybar and made them dhimmis after he had killed, tortured, raped and robbed them. On his deathbed he condemned the Jews and Christians to be banished from Arabia.

That is the Sunna. That is Islam. And that is the way Islam has treated the Jews and Christians ever since—as dhimmis. Dhimmis are Kafirs who serve Islam by submitting and laboring for Islam. If the dhimmi is subservient enough, Islam will be kind. There are no brothers of Abraham; just dhimmis to Mohammed. The root of the Israel problem is that Israel refuses to act like dhimmis.

This argument about the falseness of the Abrahamic brotherhood of Jews, Christians and Muslims is attacked by the Sunna. Another attack is to point out that a Jew or Christian is not a "real" Jew or Christian until they meet Islam's criteria. Jews must admit that the Torah is corrupt and all of the stories about Moses, David, Noah and the rest are wrong. Then Jews must accept Mohammed as the last of the Jewish prophets. Christians must deny the divinity of Jesus, His crucifixion and resurrection. Christians must also admit that the Gospels are wrong and that Mohammed is the final prophet to the Christians.

Here is the place to make the argument that in fact, the rabbi and the person who he claims is a bigot have something in common. They are both Kafirs. Of course, the rabbi is a dhimmi as well, but notice that the word is never applied to him directly. Be careful to avoid name calling, even dhimmi. Be that as it may, both are Kafirs and are not Muslims. This has consequences. If there is any brotherhood to be had, it is between Kafirs, not between Jews (or Christians) and Muslims.

- is to combat ugly anti-Muslim sentiments and make it socially intolerable.

We need to address one last bit of sophistry. The writer subtly shifts the argument about Islam to Muslims. Muslims are people and as such vary. There are 1.5 billion varieties of Muslims, but only one source of Islam. We need to stick to the study of Islam and leave Muslims out of it.

Making it socially intolerable to criticize Islam is pure social tyranny. He rejects critical thought and calls on the authorities of a fascist state to suppress ideas he does not like. Who is the true bigot?

It would seem that before a spiritual leader takes on the task of calling those who use critical thought bigots, his better task would be to seek the truth of Islamic ideology. The truth of Islam is found in the Koran, the Sunna (Sira and Hadith) and Islam's political history. As a spiritual leader, once you have mastered those texts, then speak to the issue. Until then, he should play the role of the student and stop referring to those with knowledge as bigots.

CONCLUSION

There is really only one way to learn how to use fact-based persuasion—practice. Remember, you don't need to know more than any expert you can imagine, but more that the person you are trying to persuade.

Since almost no one knows any facts, only opinions taken from the media, persuasion is much easier than you might imagine. You are not trying to change anyone's political party or how they vote, but for them to learn the truth about Islamic doctrine. If you know the facts, the way forward is easy.

CPSIA information can be obtained at www.ICGtesting.com
Printed in the USA
LVOW060457150413

329086LV00003B/166/P